Calya Journey-Wise

A Pathway for a Meaningful Life

By

Catherine L. Avizinis

ISBN: 1-4140-1670-0 (e-book)
ISBN: 1-4140-1671-9 (Paperback)

Library of Congress Control Number: 2003099863

This book is printed on acid free paper.

Printed in the United States of America
Bloomington, IN

1stBooks - rev. 03/04/04

You've decided to Journey

Now, once you're away,
Know it will take you
   a year and a day.

The way isn't easy
   and you'll oft' times feel lost
But that's part of the bargain...
   and part of the cost.

There are Guides who are
   waiting,
Companions, as well,
   with songs to be sung
   and stories to tell

To learn of your-self
FEAR DRAGONS you'll face
and with love, joy and beauty
those fears you'll replace

So Let Us Be Off!
there is much to be done!
For each soft twinkling STAR
is a Glorious Sun!

Calya Journey-wise

At the smallest level, we are all quantum VIBRATIONS. Different parts of our bodies resonate and respond to various frequencies. These are called charkas or Realms. Colors, tones, foods, herbs, essential oils, crystals and even thoughts are all VIBRATIONS which we can use to help balance the chakras.

Calya Journey-wise is a system of Metaphysical information and self guidance based on the Celtic tradition of journeying and traveling to increase knowledge and understanding of the self and how to be honorable and effective in this World and the Other. "The shamanka travels between the worlds hoping to balance and heal." Knowing yourself, identifying core beliefs, dissolving illusions and restructuring unhealthy or unwanted patterns help each Seeker to become a SOVEREIGN BEING, truly loving self, others and Life.

A Highly refined Metaphysical Healing Art based in the Celtic Tradition; using 17 vibrational frequencies, or Realms, to release, restore and revitalize your Life Force Energy with purpose. Learn to be a Sovereign Being by traveling the Realms of the Magickal land of Hammeril through Holistic Aromatherapy, guided meditation, Ritual of Movements, releasing techniques and more; all color-coded to 17 body Chakras. Seek, Find, Open and Use—on your Journey towards wellness, Comfort and Joy! At the Celtic Moon, home base for the Calya lines; Treatments, Products, a School of Metaphysical Arts and Certifications are available.

* 17 colors, different frequencies and attributes.
* 17 Energy houses to balance, relax, restore and revive.
* 17 Realms through which you will have marvelous journeys.

Our body acts as an energy transmuter…gathering in all the wondrous cosmic, Universal energies which are constantly flowing into and around us. How we use, manifest and emanate them is our choice, and we need to make and informed one. Many things are the same for all of us; that is why the system works. However, we are each a unique being with fascinating facets and fractured flaws and, therefore, our own unique Journey.

Journey-wise gives us each a map to follow. Using the system daily, enables you to participate in your own life; seek, find, open and use your own "secret color-coded message"; your map of the pathway you setup in the before time to help you learn the lessons you came here to learn.; and to arrive at your destination, your Destiny. Take one step and then another and walk until you arrive!

Coming soon!!! **Calya's Chronicles.** The novel which takes you into the Realms of Hammeril in search of the Wise Ways with Calya, Delania, Dourstan, Dithero and Non. Look for it soon! PLUS-Calya's Pendulum…, how to construct your pendulums color chart and use it in your Journey work.

Table of Contents

c. or specific for breathing rituals

Always follow the advice of your Healthcare Provider. I make no medical claims and this following information should not be misunderstood as such. Catherine Avizinis, Calya Aromatherapy and Calya Journey-wise and their affliated companies and persons are not responsible for misuse of this book, system or information, nor for allergic or adverse reactions incurred as a result of use. Not for use on children or sensitive, or delicate individuals. Pregnant or lactating women should consult their physician.

How To Use This Workbook

You will need a beautiful Journal in which to record your incredible adventures. A special, decorated one or a spiral bound notebook, whatever works best for you. Date your entries, you'll be glad when you reread.

1. Determine your "color coded message" what color are you "in?" Do this by the "Throw your stones in the Fountain" meditation or a passport—note the color in your book. Do this every day; this is your personal color-coded map.

2. Check this color against any changes or discomforts you may be feeling in your body. Use the Body Chart to confirm. If there is more than one—work with the area of your stone-color and know that the day's color work is what you need to do to help the body's discomfort de-tangle.

3. Now turn to the balance line Transmuting Chart. Read across your color and find where you fall in that Realm today. If you are Balanced or Too little, Depleted—add the color; Too Much, or Excessive, add the Compliment. (See Map and chart to bring you back to a more balanced place.) Try to become familiar with all the Realms, where they are on the map and how they relate to your body areas.

4. Use Foods to support this action of balancing as well as clothing, accessories, and the anointing oil blend in your color of the day. These will all help you Journey this Realm

by aligning your inner, outer and otherworldly energies and assisting in the alchemy—changes you are trying to make during your stay in this Realm.

5. Review the Ritual Movement that corresponds to the color— use this to "Dance-enhance" your alignment when you are ready. Do the Ritual Movement Exercises each day to help keep your total being in tune.

6. Now read through the Realm Quest Chapter of your color. Remember, if you started in one but found it was too excessive and are needing its opposite/ compliment—work with the one you need. By now, you should be identifying the specifics in your own life that, at this present time, relate to this Realm. Then deeply and honestly answer the quest questions in your Journal. These are the issues/ imbalances you are ready to work on at this time. Remember not to concern yourself with other aspects today; you just don't have the energy! Only do the work of the Realm you are in for this given message; soon you will have found more of a balance in that realm. Sometimes you will remain in a color for days and at other times your color may actually change during the day. Go with the flow. This might be a good time to do a Passport to help redefine your quest.

If at any time you just can't bear to go behind the Waterfall and into the cave, you are definitely in gray...don't go...do the Brymn work. If you happen to miss a day or two, you've missed an opportunity to work on that particular piece of your Grand Puzzle, but it's all a part of your Journey! Comfort and Joy! Safe Passage, O, Seeker!

Participate

Which color is active in your energy field?

Throw your stones in the Fountain and it will be revealed!

Find your color follows:

Throw your stones in the Fountain

Relax and do some deep tummy breathing... let your arms and shoulders feel like melting wax, softening and warm...let your legs and thighs feel heavy where you sit...we are beginning the Ritual which will take you on your Journey Through all of the Realms...see nothing but swirls of the silvery gray mists before your mind's eye...breathe a deep breath of the moment with me and deeper we go...entering the subconscious and with the next breath the mists begin to swirl and dance away and you find yourself at the Brymn Waterfall... roaring out of the side of the craggy gray Mountain tumbling into the pool and slipping away into the woods...there are boulders and there is dirt beneath your feet and you can see that in the back of the waterfall is a cave... carefully climb over the huge boulders and get in back of the waters...feel the spray on your face and hear the roar loudly in your ears...step into the cave, smell the dark dampness and the dirt... see the droplets on the grasses and tiny leaves of the plants clinging there. Turn to look back at the soft blue/gray/green waters...a veil over the mouth of the cave.

Take a deep breath and turn into the cave; you see that it is not just a cave but a Tunnel...long, dark with the brightest light at the end. Head carefully toward that brightest light and as you step out into it; it takes a moment for your eyes to adjust. See then that you are in a woodland meadow...golden grasses up to your waist, a warm sun, a glorious blue sky...and at a distance from you is an Ancient Dark Forest...over to the right side is an abandoned walled Garden...head now towards this Garden...take your time...feel the swish of the grasses against your hands... push the creaking gate open; it wobbles, half off it's hinges. Enter...there are every flower and herb imaginable all jumbled and tumbled with weeds and ivies and vines...see them...all their varied colors...smell the heady perfume released by the warmth of the sun...a bee buzzes...and a butterfly catches your eye...walk along down pathways, stepping over and on the plants which have escaped the confines of their beds long ago...feel it all...then again you hear the splash of water... you instinctively know the right path to take... turn down that path, walking strongly and purposefully. You come to a wondrous Fountain tossing plumes of water high into the air and the droplets cascades down like strings of crystal beads shimmering in the brilliant sun.........watch it...it is mesmerizing...

On your belt there hangs a pouch...reach into the pouch and there find a handful of tiny stones...toss that handful of tiny stones into the water and behold their color.........see it, perceive it hold it in your minds eye. This is your unique color-coded message today from your Inner self. The Self which is always connected to the Higher Consciousness and will guide you safely through the Magickal Land of Sammeril...sit down on the edge of the Fountain's pool and let the sun bake warmly into your clothing and on into your back...let it energize and revitalize you ...you see that the mists are closing in around your feet and legs to shut down the inner connection and you resolve to not neglect this part of the meditation... You feel accomplished...you have your Color-coded message...you feel purposeful. You are on the first step of your Journey... the mists swirl in higher and higher up around your legs and body—neck and shoulders—up over your head, until the whole scene is closed down and you are back in your own space...take your time, begin to move your hands and feet... and with a few deep breaths you have returned from Brymn Waterfall in Sammeril...Safe Passage, Wanderer...Comfort and Joy...oh Seeker...

(For each of the REALM MEDITATIONS start with this same Ritual...check the Map of the Realms to see in which direction you need to travel...then when you come out into the Brightest Light Your horse____(name it), will be waiting for you...greet it warmly, noting how it is "dressed" and then mount up and ride away to your Realm Adventure...Try to see the landscape change as you ride. When you arrive, there will always be someone there to take care of your horse; then you can pick up the Releasing Meditation from there. (Closing down the scene the with swirls of gray sparkling mists is very important. It prevents your subconscious from sneaking into your conscious thoughts and causing confusions!)

Continue on your life long Journey to wholeness and see the magick happen. Using colored pencils, why not color in the chart and map each time you visit a realm! All of the full color chapter illustrations and any of the products and supplies you may need to support your Journey are available from your local shops and bookstores and Celtic Moon. And at 1-800-321-8725, ex 205 Po box 802, Hope Valley, RI. 02832-0802 pelhamgrayson.com

Always, Calya Journey-wise is not a substitute for professional counseling or the advice of your Healthcare Provider. Always follow the advice of your Healthcare Provider. I make no medical claims and this following information should not be misunderstood as such. Catherine Avizinis, Calya Aromatherapy and Calya Journey-wise and their affliated companies and persons are not responsible for misuse of this book, system or information, nor for allergic or adverse reactions incurred as a result of use. Not for use on children or sensitive, or delicate individuals. Pregnant or lactating women should consult their physician.

Calya Journey-wise Passport

Use a passport when you feel uncertain about your issues or when you are beginning a new Journey with a new set of circumstances.

Name_____ Date_____

Last Journey_____

1, Reason: Why do you wish to travel? What is the problem?...the issue?...the Question? What needs to be resolved? Is there a specific incident that sparked this?

2. Land or Sea: Will you be taking a sea voyage or an overland journey?

Land-Yang	Sea-Yin
The Quest to bring into reality truths and qualities learned. Manifesting the deep inner self in the outer world. Living effectively by opening and using all the treasures. Implementing solid reality of what is desired.	The Quest to find hidden mysteries, uncovering truths about the self, deep Meanings and real desires. Sailing uncharted waters to seek out and find answers and secrets to bring them home.

3. Name of Ship or Horse_____
   (name must contain "Sun" and/or "Moon.")
   Sun=Yang energies activated in drive—outward, fast, expansive, hot
   Moon=Yin energies activated in drive—inward, slow, careful, cool

4. Describe Ship or Horse: colors, trappings, decorations. Translate these with Journeywork color information. This will help you to understand which energies Predominate.

5. Home Port: Describe the place you "live in" now. Why do you need to leave this Place? What is the difficulty or discomfort? Describe it as an imaginary village and name it with a whimsical descriptive name.

6. Destination: Where do you wish to go? What is it you hope to find? What is the ideal situation, the best solution? What are you looking for? What would be the worst fear?
   Name this place.

Use this as a point of departure for the next phase of your journey.

Body Realms

Is there discomfort, change or a new attention in your body?

Starting at your feet and moving upward, think about each part of your body. Are there aches/pains? New Injuries? Old complaints? Perhaps there is an area you rarely think about. OR has there recently been a change connected to a body area?   New shoes? =Black, new hairstyle=pink, even your car (an extension of self) breaking down = red. Weight gain or loss in an area? (Fat is stored energy!) These will help you to understand your knots and confirm your work. Doing conscientious work may help you to relieve these distortions and stresses and ultimately feel better.

An alternate method of checking Body Realms would be to imagine a large screen sifting through your body from feet to the top of your head. Through where in your body is it difficult to pass the screen? Are there any objects you are collecting in your screen? These can be very helpful symbols of what ails you. Now turn the page and check the charts.

COLOR	BODY AREA	ATTRIBUTES
WHITE	ABOVE CROWN	Oneness, the All, stillness, belonging
PINK	CROWN	Sovereignty, own regal realm, self-determination, dignity
VIOLET	BROW	Gratitude, realignment, calm, clear, reassess, homeward, belief
PURPLE	EYES/EARS/NOSE	Raw emotions, intuitions, claires, wisdom, feelings justified, psychic powers
INDIGO	MOUTH/JAW/OCCIPITAL	Will/choice of methods of articulating self, imagination, power of thoughts
BLUE	THROAT/NECK	Energy to express the self, truth, joy measure and worth, opinion
AQUA	SHOULDERS	Receive without guilt, pampering, care, relax, play, rejuvenate, nurtured
GREEN	CHEST/ARMS	Giving and receiving things, love, acceptance, encouragement, validation, healing action
LIME	XIPHOID	Manifesting, re-coup, digest, striving
YELLOW	SOLAR PLEXUS	New thoughts, instinct, expands awareness, self-permits, self –respects, enlightenment
PEACH	MID-ABDOMEN	Innate fears, pride, self-defense, self protection, immune,
ORANGE	LOWER ABDOMEN	Wants/needs/ desires take form, intentions, vocation, waiting?
RED	PELVIS	Creativity, raw drive, pure Life Force, sexual energies, motives
BURGUNDY	THIGHS	Making a stand, battle, power reserves, honor, strength, strategy, confrontation
BROWN	KNEES	Stability through flexibility, records, books, acknowledging another's sovereignty
BLACK	FEET	Journey, grounding of excess, willingness to leave mark in world, illusions
GRAY	ALL OVER	Fogginess, confusion, toxins, flu, wounds, need rest, retreat

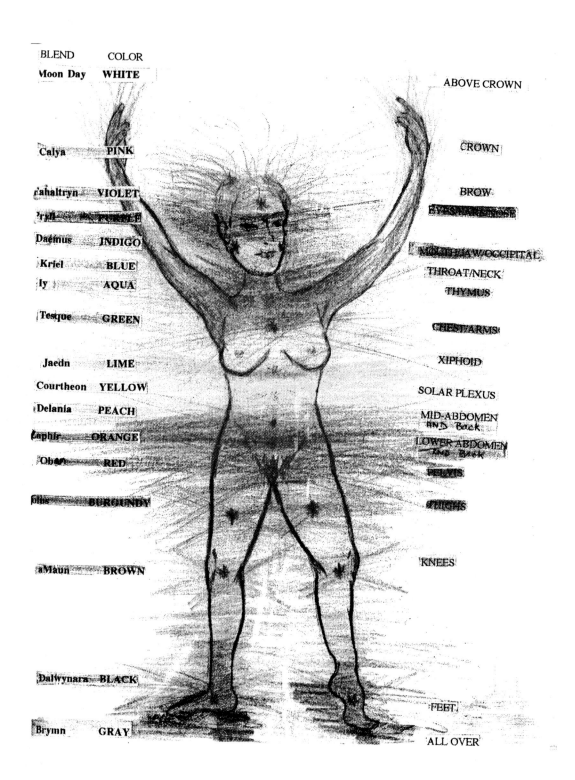

BLEND	COLOR
Moon Day	WHITE
Calya	PINK
rahaltryn	VIOLET
Pryl	PURPLE
Daemus	INDIGO
Kriel	BLUE
ly	AQUA
Tesque	GREEN
Jaedn	LIME
Courtheon	YELLOW
Delania	PEACH
Caphir	ORANGE
Oban	RED
llis	BURGUNDY
aMaun	BROWN
Dalwynara	BLACK
Brymn	GRAY

ABOVE CROWN

CROWN

BROW

EYES/EAR/NOSE

MOUTH/JAW/OCCIPITAL

THROAT/NECK

THYMUS

CHEST/ARMS

XIPHOID

SOLAR PLEXUS

MID-ABDOMEN
AND Back

LOWER ABDOMEN
AND Back

PELVIS

THIGHS

KNEES

FEET

ALL OVER

Compensate

Balance is not a
Rigid point but a *flow*

Refining extremes to
a vibrational Glow!

the TWO Headed Dragons

Fears help keep us balanced

Transmuting Extremes

To find your current position, read along the Balance Line of the appropriate color. You will feel in the middle, balanced; or perhaps in one of the fears, slightly imbalanced; or completely depleted or completely extreme. If you are balanced or on the yin-depleting side, use that color. If you are on the yang-excessive side, use the opposite. Find this by using the map and the chart next to it. This chart will give you the opposite and the Realm and aromatherapy blend, as well. If when reading your Balance Line you feel ythat you are in all the categories then use that color, you are trying to balance.

This is a very important step when doing your Journey-work. Don't assume that because your head aches that you are automatically in purple or pink; or that if your "bad knee" is acting up that you must be in brown. You must first find the color coded message and then find yourself on the Balance Line to be sure that you are using the correct vibrational frequency, the most helpful one, to address the energy distortion you may be feeling.

As with any system, Calya Journey-wise will result in the best work if you don't leave out any of the steps. Be completely honest with yourself; remembering that you are dealing with how you feel today, not in general. Using the spiritual vibrational frequency that is readily available to you today. You are helping you, and isn't that wonderful?

DEPLETED	FEAR	BALANCED	FEAR	EXCESSIVE
		GRAY		
Collapse into self	Being Well, lack of attention, not having wound Badge	Retreat	Acknowledging real wounds	Avoidance
		BLACK		
Scattered, lacking direction	Being dull	Grounded	Being crazy	Inertia, Same old rut
		BROWN		
Rigid, unyielding	Being conquered, a pushover	Stability, Flexibility	Not being accepted	Weak kneed, can't stand
		BURGUNDY		
Afraid to stand for feelings	Being attacked, deconstruction	Honorable Warrior	Not winning, reconstruction	Confrontational, always right
		RED		
Dull, Lack of drive, fatigue	Being out of bounds	Creative motives	Being Restricted	Indiscriminant expressions of the creative self
		ORANGE		
Not admitting wants, needs, or desires	Being needy, demanding	Forming authentic self	Being inconsequential	Aggression, overwhelming others
		PEACH		
Assuming no one will ever help me	No one wanting to help	Charming and Disarming	I can't help myself	Assuming all want to assist, always
		YELLOW		
No desire to change	Change means I was wrong before	Expansion of boundaries	Being narrow minded	Overextended, diffused No self-limiting
		LIME		
Not trying for anything	Not ever getting what you want	Manifesting	Not ever getting what you want	Forcing, out of step, frustrated

Transmuting Extremes

DEPLETED	FEAR	BALANCED	FEAR	EXCESSIVE
		GREEN		
Don't feel ever receiving	Being hurt	Structuring healing acceptance validation	Hurting others	Save world or someone
		AQUA		
Never take what really want, self martyrdom	Won't be allowed to have own way	Nurturing Play	Won't be allowed to have own way	Take what want anytime but blame others
		BLUE		
Low self worth, drowning	Being less than	Building the true, deep self	Being overlooked	Tell all to all, all the time
		INDIGO		
Pulling back aloof, self protect	Being ignored, not heard	Articulation imagination	Being imposed upon	Imposing will on other
		PURPLE		
See only tangible, emotional void	Own power	Emotion feelings intuition	Being beyond self, trusting	Justice in own hands
		VIOLET		
No belief in the Super natural	Changing mind, acceptance	Gratitude, re-alignment	Not feeling passionate	Head in clouds, live only dreams
		PINK		
Won't assume Regal Dignity	Being self sufficient	Sovereignty, self-direction	Rights will be usurped	Won't allow others sovereignty
		WHITE		
Denying self access to Super natural	Being alone	Stillness, Magickal alchemy	Being absorbed	Must stay in control of all

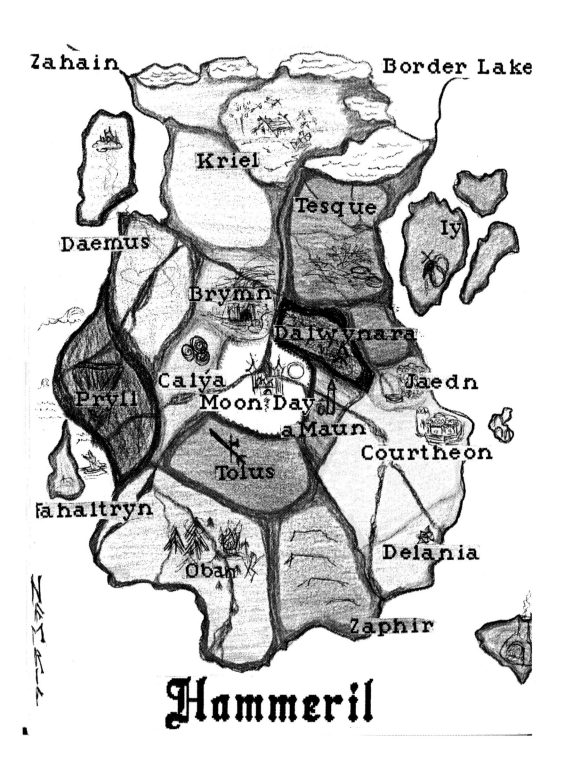

Zahain Border Lake

Kriel

Tesque

Iy

Daemus

Brymn

Dalwynara

Jaedn

Calya

Pryll

Moon Day

aMaun

Courtheon

Tolus

Fahaltryn

Delania

Oban

Zaphir

Hammeril

Color	Body Ailment	Blend	Balances	If Excessive Use
White	Above Head	**MOON DAY** For Stillness	Belonging & Longing	Black Dalwynara
Pink	Crown of Head	**CALýA** For Sovereignty	Self Reliance	Brown aMaun
Violet	Brow	**FAHALTRYN** For Gratitude	Changing the Mind	Lime Jaedn
Purple	Eyes/Ears/Nose	**PRYLL** For Power	Feelings/Intuition	Yellow Courtheon
Indigo	Occipital/Jaw	**DAEMUS** For Imagination	Choices	Peach Delania
Blue	Throat/Neck	**KRIEL** For Joy	Self Worth	Orange Zaphir
Aqua	Shoulders	**IY** For Guilt	Work/Play	Burgundy Tolus
Green	Chest/Arms	**TESQUE** For Love	Giving/Receiving	Red Oban
Lime	End of Breastbone	**JAEDN** For Frustration	Striving	Violet Fahaltryn
Yellow	Solar Plexus Stomach	**COURTHEON** For Boundaries	Expansion	Purple Pryll
Peach	Upper Abdomen & Back	**DELANIA** For Fears	Self-Defense	Indigo Daemus
Orange	Lower Abdomen & Back	**ZAPHIR** For Purpose	Wants/Needs/Desires	Blue Kriel
Red	Pelvis/Groin	**OBAN** For Creativity	Motives	Green Tesque
Burgundy	Thighs	**TOLUS** For Honor	Warrior Strength	Aqua Iy
Brown	Knees	**aMAUN** For Stability	Flexibility	Pink Calýa
Black	Feet	**DALWYNARA** For Direction	Excesses	White MoonDay
Gray	All over	**BRYMN** For Confusion	Exhaustion	Gray Brymn

Regulate

...with the needed
energies *Y*our-self
surround...

...stimulate, support,
soothe, nurture, ground.

FOODS AND CRYSTALS

Color	Foods	Crystals
Gray	anything you feel able to eat	plain gray stones, kyanite
Black	coffee, blk walnuts, mushrooms, chocolate	smoky quartz, hematite, onyx
Brown	nuts, peanuts, potatoes, tea	tiger's eye, petrified wood, amber
Burgundy	combine browns and reds, apples etc.	garnet, ironstone, jaspers
Red	tomatoes, red cabbage, red onions, red peppers	ruby, red jasper,
Orange	oranges, mangoes, carrots, yams	carnelian, orange calcite, red rock
Peach - combine oranges and yellows, peaches		peach dolomite, feldspar, Mongolian salt
Yellow	bananas, lemons, eggs, squash	sulfur, yellow calcite, gold
Lime	combine yellows and greens	peridot, chrysocola, prehnite
Green	green vegs, (eat stalks, leaves, flowers) herbs/teas,	Tourmaline, jades, emerald
Aqua	combine greens and blues	apatite, aquamarine
Blue	all animal protein,(meats)	blue calcite, turquoise, denim lapis
Indigo	milk, butter, yogurt, ice cream	lapis, sodalite, indigoite
Purple	grains, pasta, breads, berries, grapes	amethyst, iolite, tanzanite

Violet	sugars, pastries, candies, alcohol	nlepidolite, lt amethyst
Pink	some special treat	rose quartz, sugilite, rhodacrosite, tourmaline
White	fresh water, clean air, sun/moonshine	quartz, diamonds, herkimers, milky qrtz

Calya-Cise

Calya Journey-Wise course will help you to expand your understanding of the Realms, the meaning of the colors, the quest Questions and how to travel.

Comfort and Joy ... Safe Passage.

Home Stance—feet aligned under shoulders, knees softly flexed, spine lengthened, pelvis forward, chin tucked, shoulders back, chest open, and arms long with palms up in front of lower abdomen with thumbs closed. All movements are done in a slow, relaxed way—with deep breathing helping to move energies. Work up to 100ct. unless specified.

1. Black—*Begin walking*...willing to journey. Leave mark. Are you blaming another? Look in the mirror. 50 Yin toe/heel... 50 Yang heel /toe...Breathe.

2. <u>Yellow</u>—*Thru the Gate*... make the decision to Journey. Enter into participation in your <u>own</u> <u>life</u>...put down your box. Slowly roll spine up, knees softly flexed, think of all the colors as your hands pass their body areas.

3. <u>Grey</u>—*Salutation*...<u>acknowledge</u> there is a problem or issue, something beyond what you know...something outside and inside of you. Be ready to find the new box. Repeat #2, 3x only flow more quickly and swing arms to back over head when bent down.

4. <u>Purple/Indigo</u>—*Searches*...seeking direction, asking and articulating, ask for help. Where to go...colors. Knees flexed, pelvis forward, arms long, palms up, stretch neck by looking slowly side to side then up and down and holding. Relaxed posture—Smile!

5. <u>Blue</u>—*Seasons and Cycles*...observing and learning the <u>patterns</u> in your life...universal truths. <u>How you fit</u>...you're not all that important. Switching weight from front to back with bent legs, arms circle like passing a stick or a large ball. Breath.

6. <u>Aqua</u>—*Wings*...you ARE the most important thing in your universe...your journey, destiny... let <u>self worth soar</u>!!!! 1.) Relaxed posture, lift arms to shoulder height and rotate all the way forward and then back—continue adding head, neck, shoulders and torso—always keeping pelvis forward. 2.) Rotate arms forward raise shoulders to ears and swing back trying to touch relaxed hands.

7. <u>Green</u>—*Yin/Yang*...hoping to <u>balance</u> and <u>heal</u> <u>self</u>, <u>others</u>, realms. Merge extremes to balance point, flow. Relaxed posture, knees bent, side bends with pelvis forward arm stretches up, out, over. Left then right—very slow stretches.

8. <u>Peach</u>—*Gargoyle*... Break down old to create new, what is your position of belief? What are you guarding so fiercely? What is you <u>inate</u> <u>fear</u>? Crouch down with your heels flat and arms between your legs, then drop your head and straighten the knees. Repeat three times and growl!

9. <u>Orange</u>—*Ocean Depths*...Wants, needs, desires, what's the difference? Pull them up into consciousness and pull up strengths from deep down inside. Lay on the floor—open mid-back (see#2 to open mid back) with head raised, chin tucked and legs bent but relaxed. Round up and softly pull the small of your back into the floor, then progress to legs lifted and work up to 100ct.

10. <u>Pink</u> –*Double Helix*...Wring out deep life force. <u>Define your realm</u> ...the worst/best? Move into action, make power usable. Lying flat on your back—arms bent out at shoulders. Roll bent right leg over left leg and relax into stretch. Deep breaths release tapped excess energies. Reverse. Breath pink out the top of your head.

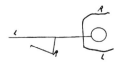

11. <u>Red</u>—*Attitude*...<u>M</u>otives – make a stand for your beliefs wants/needs/desires. Lying on your side with knees slightly bent, pelvis forward and head propped on hand, use the other hand for balance and bring your top bent knee to your face. Then, push to it back keeping it as close to your bottom leg as you can and always pelvis forward. Three times and reverse.

12. <u>V</u>iolet—*Moon Faces*...Changes are good, show and know and accept your different aspects. Refine the self and define your realm. Sit up—bend the right knee flat to the floor with the other knee in front of the body. Bend the left leg upright crossing over the right. The right arm pulls up and over the left leg to stretch and turn the back pulling with the left hand. Count to 50 and reverse.

13. <u>Brown</u>—*Flying Horse*...<u>Stability</u> through <u>flexibility</u>. Mount up... what's your strategy, plan? Sit with legs out, bend your right knee in, and turn to face it—relax your body down over the bent leg. Keep your left leg out straight in back. Count to 10, raise your head, place palms back to bent knee—slowly arch back lifting one arm at a time over your head. Count to 10 and reverse.

14. <u>Burgundy</u>—*Battle*...willing to <u>fight</u> for yourself, realm, allies...who will be defeated, are you ready to be responsible? Moving from #13 sitting with your left knee bent in front of your body, bend the right knee flat to the floor out to the right side—pelvis pulled forward. Rotate your right leg in your hip, lift up two inches and push back slightly with little pulses. Lean to your side for balance eventually working to sitting upright. Work to 100. Reverse.

15. <u>Pink</u>—*Protect*...stand by your decisions, your self and your allies...who are they? You better know and be honorable when dealing with them. Moving from #14, leaving your right knee bent, bring your right leg bent upright and lift all the body weight up and forward onto the left bent leg. Stretching torso down to the floor, count to 10 and Reverse.

16. <u>Lime</u>—*Openness*...Ready to manifest what you truly wanted from the beginning with all the layers peeled away and fears faced and over-come, reach out to help another! Sitting with your legs out, hug your liver with your left arm and bend to the left with the right arm stretching up and over. 50 count. Reverse, hugging your spleen with your right arm and the left arm

goes up and over. 50 count. Then bring your feet together in front of you with straight legs and stretch your arms up, out, and over pulling your head down and elbows up and out to open the mid-back. 50 ct.

17. <u>Peach/Pink</u>—*Shiela na Gig*... Pride in self and accomplishments. Remembering that Pride keeps you fighting even when there is no cause. Sitting very upright, draw your knees up as tightly as possible and wrap your arms inside of your thighs and under your knees to grasp the shins. Stretch, grow and breath. Hold for 10.

18. <u>White</u>—*Beyond the Beyond*... See self as part of the web of life, part of the whole, the network...my Journey matters to the All. Sit with legs out, bracing your body weight on a straightened right arm, and swing the left arm wide over your head and lift your body. Hold for five and reverse and repeat.

Translate

Relax and Remember
when you Journey into *you*
This is no competition
& the messages are True

No, It's not the thoughts

You think that Reveal

but the *tiny flutter of image,*
& what you truly Feel

Chapter work follows:

Realm Quick Questions

Gray...What is the wound? What are the toxins? ...The confusions? Do I feel lost, abandoned?

Black...What shadow stalks me? What do I find annoying/hurtful in others? Am I progressing on my path of true desire?

Brown...What was written, agreed upon, in the "before time"? Will I bow to the previous agreement to accomplish the lesson I chose to learn?

Burgundy...What is the Battle? What needs to be overcome? Do I know the enemy?

Red...What are my true motives? What is moving me? ...Help and Harmony or Hindrance and Harm?

Orange...For what in this life do I wait? Who says? What do I intend?

Peach...What is the innate fear? Have I defended myself well in the past? Is it still necessary to defend myself?

Yellow…Do my beliefs match my actions? What is forcing me to change? Who is my soul mate?

Lime…What do I need to digest? What is the frustration? For what am I striving? Will I choose to manifest now?

Green…Whom do I love? Am I giving and receiving? What do I want to restructure?

Aqua…Do I need nurturing and pampering? Why do I feel no one will? Am I afraid to ask? What would be good play?

Blue…Who am I in my family chain? What are the genetic behavioral patterns? How is my timing?

Indigo…Have I overstepped a bound? …stepped too soon? Have I kindly set Boundaries for others and kept them clear?

Purple …Who or What has hurt me? How do I feel…really? Do I have Intuitions/feelings on this issue? What would be justice?

Violet…What did I want? How do I (you) like me now? Can I be grateful for what "is"?

Pink…Have I become my truer self? Where is my Realm? Is there more to come? Am I allowing others to reach for sovereignty?

White…Do I feel still? Can I see the magickal changes happening around me?

Brymn H

Gray Allover   **Muzzy Retreat**
Cloak   **Hagal=Chaos**
Mountain Mists, Nargylls

Confusion, Toxins, Disease, Wounded, Poison Realm of Muzzy-
we feel it all over: Foggy head, sad, depressed, depleted, nervous,
exhaustion, wounded and full of poisons.

Retreat is a viable option, in fact, the best act6ion at this time.
You are not at a point of moving ahead at this time!

The Wounds, Sadness and Malaise need to be acknowledged.
Many things may be "wrong" or unsatisfactory; draining your
Life Force; poisoning your system and your efforts.

What are your issues? Wounds? Hurts? Name them. What
is it you do not want to face? Name it—then don't face it.

Your energy is in back flow—your cycle is in retrograde. You
need help—realize this, admit this, speak it out loud; and then
later in your Journey, when your timing is aligned, help will be
there.
Sometimes when in gray you will feel just too overwhelmed to
Journey or get well. At other times you will avoid stopping or
being alone at all cost so you won't have to acknowledge the
issue or real hurt. Seek balance.

The Road is fogged over—you need to make camp. Find
shelter and retreat and rest deeply. No need to progress on your
journey today—were to begin to fix what is wrong? Don't
concern your mind and heart today. Rest—pull back—only
NAME the wound and journal it. It is deep and poisons your life.
Name it and know it. Retreat, you are overwhelmed. This is a
deep moment of identifying a root cause of energy matrix

distortion, one of the tangled knots in the web of your life's energy. Herein lies a scar.

Today, however, just wrap your cloak of invisibility around you and blend into your surroundings. Do only those things you absolutely feel you can. Does your Reality seem out of order? Turned in on you? Have you caused another's confusion? Universal energies are not in a forward flow for you now. Rest— stay quiet. Retreat. Disappear. Let the Gentle Mists of invisibility enclose you, and hide you in Reality. We need these times to help us pinpoint issues. Soon the shift will come and end the Chaos.

Dalwynara

Black Feet   **Mirrors**
Blacksmith—Castle Mirrors   **Rad=Journey**
Sacred Path

Grounding Excess, Cycles end, Shadow Self, Curse Cures,
Reality Restores, Reflections

All things contain all things. There is a Microcosm and a Macrocosm and each Reflects energies of the other. The more Honorably you walk on your Path the more honor will be expected from your self.

The Law of Triples applies. That which you create and put out into the energy flow will be drawn back to you with three times the power. If you put out fear you will become three times more fearful. If you put out revenge you will become three times more vengeful. If you put out kindness you will be able to become three times more kind! There is a shadow self which haunts your inner castle. Your fears, yes, but moreover, your failings and selfish decisions, the parts of you that you deem unworthy, unpardonable, treacherous or unacceptable.
Sometimes in black you will feel lost and that your life has no purpose. At other time your purpose will seem as drudgery and you'll feel that you simply must just crawl out of yourself! Seek balance.

What do you see in others that is irritating or unacceptable? When in Black, it is a mirror. You are seeing yourself reflected and you don't like it.

This is the Reality of your Journey. Face yourself! When you do, the Excess of energy and emotion will be grounded out your legs and feet and absorbed by Mother Earth the Primal Goddess Yin, because Excess extremes would cause you to stray from your Authentic Path.   Recognizing the truth will keep you balanced and grounded and enables you to continue with honor and humility. Your direction becomes clear and your path of Enlightened Evolution will then be before you.

Am I using all the Natural means at my disposal to achieve Super Natural? ...And all the Super Natural to Create Natural? Do your Transmuting alchemy, spell work, prayer rituals and ceremony to honor your Life (lives) and the alchemical alignments working with you for your Path of Destiny. Recognize past life connections and shadows—Totem animals, Spirit Guides. What is my True Path in this part of my Journey? Take one step and then another—walk until you arrive.

aMaun

Brown Knees   **Meanings**
Tower of Records   **Odal=security**
Life changing

Stability through Flexibility, Harvest Home, What is written?
Information in My Book

What is written in my book? What were the contracts and agreements in the before time? You have the Regal Right to know. Acknowledge who you are—really. As you become your truest self with fears released and twisted beliefs smoothed out the Browns will keep you stable through being flexible.

Where is Harvest Home? That Safe Place of reaping and success? Your Journey is a unique expression fulfilling those contracts and agreements, learning those chosen lessons—sorting out what fears twist the self into a distorted tangle instead of the beautifully intricate knot work expression of your True and Sacred Path.

Sometimes when in Brown you'll feel afraid of not being accepted and then be willing to do anything to avoid being rejected. At other times you will lock up and become rigid, refusing to compromise. Seek balance.

It is written, recorded—you can know at any time, you can obtain access to your "Permanent Record" and if in Brown be able to be stable and flexible enough to Bow the knee to the honorable agreement previously made. Do you really want to know?

It is helpful to see this life changing information outside of time. We all have a Free Will and can make any choices that seem good at the moment. Through Journey-wise we want to make choices based on the Universal Principals of the best good of comfort and joy for yourself and all others concerned while following your unique Path of self-determination. This balancing, and merging become your magickal transformation, your enlightenment, accomplished with honor and Stability through Flexibility.

Tolus

Burgundy thighs   **Mettle**
Battle Hammer   **Thorn=Destruction**
                                                  Make a Stand

Power Reserves, Strategy, Attack or be Attacked, Allies, Battle,
Deep Strength

This is War! The old patterns, which do not serve you well, are not bringing about your health, happiness and wholeness; need to be broken down. Do you know the Enemy? Who/What is the thorn in your side? What Pattern in or outside of Your Self needs to be smashed or battled against with honor, dignity and skillful strategy?

You will always know your own next move when dealing with yourself others. When dealing with others, skill is always more important than might. Staying in control of the situation by walking away is honorable. Wanting the Victory of Truth and Honor is NEVER wrong. To be a successful Warrior Chieftain/Chieftana, you must know yourself and your adversary.

Sometimes when in Burgundy you will fear confrontation because of the breaking down process that will happen, the crumbling away. At other times it will be the replacement that you will fear. Wanting only you to be right means no compromise and then you become the "Thorn"! Seek balance.

Stand your ground; use your thigh energy to pull circumstances in your favor. Is your cause just and are your strategies Honorable? Check this now. Do they serve Justice, Truth, Honor, Love and Compassion for ALL concerned including you? There are some things for which it is worth fighting!

Burgundy gives you fast, strong action for defense and offense. Break it down! Conquer it! Deconstruct to Reconstruct. Fierce Power, quick changes, explosive energies needed to overcome.

Don't store away grudges, deal with them as needed. Focus on winning the outcome of your desires and crumble away all else. If you lie to yourself about your motive, the destruction you put out will 3X wash back over you and you will become capable of three times the destruction. Draw up the Sovereign Dignity to make a fierce Battle for your honorable cause and then fight until you win; always remembering who will loose and the price they will pay. Only fight until it is over; stay true to your allies and be sure of the standard you bear as you make a stand.

Oban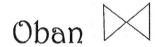

Red Pelvis   **Movement**
Fire   **Daeg=Immediacy**
                                                  Life Force

Physical Disciplines, Ambitions, Motives, Move, Raw Energy Force, Sex Drive, Creativity

Raw Life Force, the Power and Ambition to Create and Sexual urgency define this Realm.   This raw life force is in great abundance in Youth.   If directed with discipline one can achieve great creations including a new <u>life</u> (baby).   But create other things as well; create yourself and the life you choose.   You must care for, replenish, keep healthy, your physical self as well as Soul and Spirit.   Movements (exercise, ritual dance) and eating well are as important to a balanced Spiritual Journey as are meditation and doing interior inspection and disciplines.

Do you need to eat differently?   Move differently?   Take supplements?   Learn to access and use your Life Force energy (charka energies).   Your <u>power</u> may be used for Help and Harmony or Hindrance and Harm, which do you choose?   Know you can affect other energies because you exist; because Life Force flows through you.

Sometimes when in Red you will feel tired and drained because denying your creative fire means of expression, due to real or imagined rules, will surely deaden it. At other times denying it will make you rebellious and indiscriminant.   Seek balance.

Red Life Force is Potential.   It is Fiery, Potent Power.   Will you choose to wield your power with discipline and honor; being mindful of the results of your actions?   Check your motives.

What is the cause of your move? What moves you? Know your body and what it needs and what it can and can't do. Your Body can direct your Powers and energies in very purposeful ways. Sexuality can be used to release incredible waves of your orgasmic energy (Tantric Sex) for creating incredible achievements.

Learn the disciplines to create with honor and purpose and create Comfort and Joy for yourself and others. What do you expect to happen? Remember your wants should never over shadow another's needs. Be very clear; don't take your power lightly or your Body for granted. Keep Creating, forever and today.

Zaphir

Orange Lower Abs and Back   **Mastery**
Wand   **Tyr=Victory**
                                     Authentic Self

Wants, Needs, Desires Taking Form, Art/Purpose, Vocation

Who are you supposed to be? Who do you know you are? Arc you not feeling Master/Mistress of your own fate? What is the Discontent? In orange we are ready to deal with issues involving our vocation. What did I come into this lifetime to accomplish; to show forth? What is my Art or my work or my true self, my authentic purpose for being here?

Sometimes when in Orange you won't admit your wants, needs, or desires, even to yourself; preferring to deem yourself inconsequential. At other times you'll aggressively push through anyone in your path to have your own way. Seek balance.

Am I afraid to succeed at my "dreams?" Identify Needs as absolute necessities, food, shelter, acceptance, validation, touch. Wants as specific things I'd like to obtain—this house, that necklace, this kind of partner, and Desires as dreams, ideals and goals perhaps seemingly unobtainable but they are as necessary as needs, or one will become stagnate— feel accomplished and stop reaching for ideals and dreams,— or live life feeling deadened and depressed. An excess of unused energy here a pot belly/ lower back problems! Middle years! The more you use it the more it flows, you don't use it up...the more "reasonable demand" the better.

Who says?... You can't—You shouldn't?... For what in this life do you wait? This is one of the most important questions to answer when in Orange. Permission? Someone to change?

Retirement? Stop waiting—Be your true self now! Don't be afraid to change the rules. Change, grow, evolve, succeed. Are you ready to do the work of your Journey—your task that <u>you</u> chose to accomplish in this lifetime? Admit your wants, needs and desires and sort them into columns in your Journal. There may be times you actually feel pregnant; with ideas, purpose or even literally. Then when the energies shift there can be a "labor" of bringing forth with real cramps and back pain.

Dare to make your dreams exist in reality. Take time to grow, change and form your True, Honorable, Wonderful Authentic Self.

Delania

Peach Spleen/Kidneys/Adrenals   Mien
Adornment   Elks=Good Fortune
                                       Manner of Being

Disarming, Outer shows Inner, Immune, Protect, Self Defense, Fears

Our inner selves Adorn our outer selves, showing our truth, whether we like it or not. Our fears color our whole being. Pride keeps us fighting even when there is no cause. Beware! Don't make others pay for a particular hurt in your life with which they had nothing to do; different person now...different time.

Our Immune system and adrenals help us survive—they guard us with fears and protect us with masks for self defense. When we let go of old patterns and imagined attacks our outer Mien will show this as well. Is it still necessary to defend myself—protect myself and be on my guard? Have I defended myself well in the past?

Have I learned my past Journey lessons? Is there still a threat? A battle? Or can I learn to be charming and disarming? Not having to defend my position, territory, and personal beliefs. Am I being attacked or just imagining it because I used to be attacked and so fall into a "defend myself at all cost" mechanism?

Sometime when in Peach you will fear no one will come to your aid and at other times you will assume all others will certainly want to help me and be concerned with my problems; why wouldn't they, I need help. This turns into manipulation; getting your needs met at any cost and at anyone's inconvenience. Seek balance.

Two Lessons: 1. You are the most important person in the Universe and 2. To others you are just not that important.

Am I immune to others needs?   Do I think I should be immune to struggle hardship; shouldn't have to deal with inconvenience or discomfort or illness myself? Am I willing to change my perception of myself? Am I willing to show others I mean them no harm, no threat, no competition for territory or center stage? There is no hiding truth. Try to take the spotlight off of your issues and fears and see that others have problems, too. Call off the War! It's not you or them! It takes courage to find Peace.

Courtyon

Yellow Solar Plexus Light

Matching Re-Enlightenment Instinct Action Beliefs

New thoughts, Growth, Put Down Your Box, Change, Expand, Soul Mate

Put Down Your Box (of how you think it should be). Old beliefs, old patterns, old ways of going, doing, and being have or are now crumbling away and a new day is dawning.

Something needs to change because something is forcing it to—something is not working anymore. Perhaps the situation is beyond your control—a death, a circumstance your or someone else's decision or action is forcing you to adjust who you are. Life is interrupting!

Passing through this gateway is truly the beginning of a new phase of your journey. Who are you? What do you do? Why are you here at this present point? Who do you want to be? What do you really want to do? Why have you decided to journey? What holds you back? Stops you? Has there been rejection? It is an illusion that someone else holds you back—it is always your own decision. You are not a prisoner—you are free to go. Yellow/gold is a big step of deciding things need to change and that you are willing to seek, find, open and use the information in this system to participate in your own life's Journey!

Match your outer actions to your inner beliefs. Put down everything you think you know and be ready to travel at first light. A new thought, a new way, is about to break into your Being/Instincts. Enlightenment is about to happen. A first step by you, to begin using Light. Relating to the outer world through your inner and other world self.

Sometimes when you enter Yellow you'll feel that if you change that it means your old way was wrong. At other times you'll fear appearing unwilling to change and so you'll change directions with every slight breeze that blows past. Seek balance.

Independence, co-dependence—your soul mate. Do you see your Soul Mate in another? The other with whom you wish to be filled and wish to fill. Perhaps you have even met up with your Twin Flame, the person whom embodies the energies of your other self. NO! It does not mean you should abandon your existing life to run after this person. It means your task on this part of your Journey is to seek, find, open, and use Balance to merge the extremes and stay honorable to all as you do. Learn the lessons, merge the qualities. Go! Do! Be! Use your own soul's or Soul Mate's Energy to go out and beyond. Are there missions and lessons to accomplish for the freeing of all of you!!? Put down your box, and be open!

Jaedn

Lime Xiphoid
The Well of Desire

Manifest
Nyd=Absolute
Bring Forth Now!

Re-coup losses, Balance, What You Asked For, Happening Now!

Those things which you truly, deeply and absolutely desired will be brought into Reality now—whether they were conscious or not. You've worked hard to follow the Journey Path you had set before you in the before time—you had little deaths and little accomplishments but once you shift into Lime the Real Desired change will happen. Now!

When in lime check if you have assessed your Home Port, decided to Journey, weighed the risks, counted the costs and decided you absolutely could not stay where you were. Have you traveled the Realms? Worked hard, struggled, faced realities and fear Dragons? Broke down old patterns, re-structured newness, asked for help and become self-sufficient? Called on <u>self</u> and other world guides and energies, worked on your alchemy spells, alignments and prayers? Studied and learned? Were you willing to seek, find, open and use; oh, worthy Seeker? Now manifest what you will—and pull up from the Deep Well of Desire in your own Balanced Sovereign Realm what you truly wanted all along—surprised?

Sometimes when stressed in lime it is because you can't seem to get what you want so you either feign giving up (did't want it anyway) or strive to the point of total frustration, which may cause you liver ailments, gallstones or ulcers! Seek balance.

If you have worked towards or wished for a thing or circumstance but it just doesn't seem to be manifesting it is because you say one thing but your actions "say" another and set the cosmic machinery in motion to produce something else. If you say you want to make a job change then actively look for a job, don't just complain because that only brings back a wave of your energy and you will be able to complain three times as much! ... Have three times more to complain about!!!

Your own Realm needs you—form it, govern it. Bring it forth as the kind, generous, powerful creative Regal Lord/Lady under whose rule you'd like to live. Rule it Regally, with Great Honor, Compassion, Justice, Comfort and Joy!

Tesque /\\

Green Chest and Arms   **Medicinals**
Herbs   **Mann=Relationships**
                                                   Abundance

Healing, Acceptance, Giving and Receiving, Cleansing, Love
Restructure

I love who you are. We live in a Reciprocal Universe—for every action there is an equal and opposite reaction. Green is action—the acts of validation, acceptance, giving and receiving are all HEALING; as much to the one doing them as the one receiving them. This is the Breath of Life.

The Best Medicine of Acceptance of self's and other's fascinating facets and fractured flaws is soothing and healing; brings health and wholeness; but how do we get there? Relearn truths—restructure your core beliefs, your inner workings—exam them, cleanse them, re-order them, they are the skeletal structure of your life. Realign with Mother Earth, Nature and Universal Truths that cannot be denied. Seasons, Cycles, Colors, Universal clockwork, Respect, Comfort, Joy—opposites make a whole—not wrong "<u>or</u>" right but "and." But always "harm none" stands. There is never an excuse for abuse. What are you contributing to a difficult situation? ...to a good situation?

Sometimes when in Green there will be a fear to act; either because of being hurt yourself or of hurting someone else. Don't with hold acts of love but don't use them to simply please yourself; make yourself look good to you or others. Truly give these words and actions and then let go of them. Seek balance.

Hospitality=entertaining another being—hosting and not expecting <u>another</u> to <u>be you</u>. Allow self and others to be unique without fear or aggression. Just Allow differences, opinions, goals. This takes cleansing, healing, and acceptance. Accomplish this by using all the Realm Energies available to you, your inner, outer and other world energies which you may note and admire to pattern on and boost or balance your own. Hospitality, Healing, Wholeness, restructure core beliefs. Believe the Elements and how they work together. Green is the Actions of Love and the Realm where we allow another their failings; try to find their specialness and applaud them for it! ... And if their failings have been exceedingly great; allow them to fail, and know that they have... send it over Forever Falls to be continued...on into this incredible Universe of Human Relationships.

Iy

Aqua Shoulders Thymus	Message
Essential Oils/Massage	Gyfu=Gifts
	Pamper

Nurturing, Play, Recreate, <u>Receive</u>, Be Cared For, What is the Message? Rejuvenate

The need for Play is essential. The need for (necessity for) pampering and care is universal and undeniable. There will be little joy if one is not touched and desired and made a fuss over; allowed to be the center of attention once in a while.

Getting your own way—having the say, as well as occasionally being silly and playful and irresponsible is very rejuvenating. Let your youth and vitality be restored by allowing yourself to be pampered. Why do you think no one will? Ask for it—call it in from the other world. Don't fear the rejection; look for the incoming messages and Receive them...or is your receiver hardened over from past hurts and neglects?

Begin by fully receiving compliments without guilt or embarrassment, which is really one of the masks of your pride of self worth. Be Proud of You! Not ashamed of being proud of you! You must refill your nurturing tank or you will not be able to nurture; you'll be too depleted.

Oil massage! What color is the predominant one? Aqua, wear it—teal and aqua use them. Care for yourself in all aspects, expect gifts from all places, look for them find them, care for yourself or who will? What would be good to play at today? What would be exciting? Bold? Different? Comforting? If there is no person in your life on whom you can call—call on your guides—Gods and Goddesses and make recreation time for yourself. Get away—especially to the ocean or water, a bath? Long and bubbly? A hot tub with another?

Sometime when in aqua you'll deny yourself even simple rest, food, pleasure or play, (that'll show 'em and prove how hard I work!) and at other times you'll do just as you please and be sure everyone hears just how terrible you have it and how poorly you are treated. Seek balance.

Nurture and give nourishment to all parts of you. Find the gifts others give to you each day—a compliment, letting you join in, pass in traffic, a sunrise, a night's sleep. Be assured the gifts will be flowing. Play and receive—give no thought to your Journey!

Kriel

Blue Throat/Neck
Crystals

Measure
Birkin=Rebirth
Family Chain

Energy to Express Self, Building Self-Worth, Place, Uniqueness, Timing

My turn to be _____! What a Joy! Take Time! Remember who you are genetically, a link in a chain. Unique, you are, but the same. Shared companionship is important for self worth and identity—your Family, Hometown, State, Country, Planet, Reality, and your sub-culture. Like-minded friends and acquaintances give us Power to express self, without forfeit or fear of rejection. Recognize and be recognized. Take time to mourn—then Journey on.

Mourn those who have gone on out of your life or passed on to the other world; then Journey on. Do not live in the past or the future—now exists for you as a jewel—take it. Take what you need absolutely without guilt.
Sometimes when in blue you'll fear that what you have to say or offer is not given worth or merit. At other times you'll hear yourself repeating the same information over and over again to anyone who will listen. Seek balance.

When in blue, define your genetic attributes and family history; the Family Behavioral Patterns. You are a unique combination of ancestors and it's your time to try to work it out. This is your lifetime so don't try to live out another's; not a family member's nor one of your past lives. Do <u>not</u> take more than you need, but take appropriate nourishment, time, attention, and money. Know the difference between wants, needs, and desires and adjust the amounts. Is your timing off?

Do you arrive at a point before others or are you always too late? Do you speak when you should hold back or vice versa? Do you know "your place?" Are you carrying a Burden of "what might have been if only...?"

Go to the Crystal River of Time and get a new timepiece—ancestor energies will help you to know and align with precise timing. Ask them to flow through you. Accept what you have at this time and Journey from there. Your self worth needs to be balanced by mistakes, so acknowledge them. Work on your place in Time. Eat, Drink and be Merry! Feast with Family and listen to who you are. Don't fight it—Rejoice in it!

Daemus

Indigo Pituitary/Jaw
Voice/Thoughts

Meditation
Lagu=Flow
Laughter

Extend Yourself-Be Articulate, Imagination, Wit, Tell Story

Using the gifts of the articulate self to speak; when in Indigo, talk; tell your tales. Share yourself. Extend your life to others. The will is the thing—will you or will you not, be a fool for another's heart? As above—so below, that's the way the lessons go.

Sometimes when in Indigo you'll feel you are not being heard so why bother talking. At other times you will have allowed your boundaries to be crossed and trampled so, in anger, you will want to "pay them back!" Seek balance.

Karma—What you give out comes back to you over and over and there exists reciprocative abundance between the worlds. It is time to pass through the veil to a deeper awareness. Understand that your thoughts do create your reality and that you <u>will</u> bring about what you truly believe. The lesson? Don't say one thing and mean something else; not to the people in your life nor to the spirits. It's deceitful and confusing.

Honor Energies. Talk to the Mystical Otherworldly Beings you feel are working with you and develop respectful relationships. They love rhythm and rhyme, music and dance. Tell them your stories they'll be entranced! Then if you earn their respect you will have new allies, friends and defenders—and that works both ways.

Honor each other, Entrain and Align with Universal Principles. Respecting Boundaries is so very important. Stop equating other world with spooky terror and evil—it is not. Helps are given as needed and merited. Know what you believe and believe what you know.

Never Fail in Courtesy and Hospitality! Have I over stepped a bound? Stepped too soon? Have I not set clear Boundaries and allowed others to impose on me and now I'm hurt and angry? Have I assumed others "know" or "should know" what I mean, need, want? Articulate in a new way—carefully and with imagination. Do you see the shocking horror and futility of imposing your <u>will</u> on another? Why would you want something from someone who does not want to give it to you, or to be with you? Is not aligned with you? Be polite—Don't force issues— Talk, Laugh, be witty and extend yourself, language and laughter are mystical and magickal. Meditate and extend your thoughts.

Þryll ᚠ

Purple Eyes/Ears/Nose
Music/Lightening

Music
Feoh=Hard won acquisitions
Emotions

No Competition, Music Weaves Worlds, All Claires, Psychic, Pure Passions

Harm none and do what you will. Intuition and Clairvoyance of all kinds. How do you feel? Admit it—Deep emotions and passions are the Powers of Changes and Psychic Alchemy. Learn to use your Magickal Music in a controlled way—organized purposeful, a beautiful song.

How and what you feel is expressed in the head—you know the truth through Intuition. If in Purple, believe what you feel you know; you are absolutely right, but only when you are in purple. Your Psychic energy is powerful now. Work your magick. Music is important, not musical? Use recorded music of others that expresses your feelings and enhances your powers.

Sometimes when in Purple you may fear what you might be capable of saying or doing and so close down your feelings to the point where you will feel no passion or emotions at all. At other times you'll not believe that the "authorities",(on whatever level) will be able to serve justice to suit you and try to take matters into your own hands. Seek balance.

As the Life Force Power flashes through your system, your passion or strength-of-feeling gives more power to your expression and psychic alchemy. This is where you add your Personal Powers to the Grand flow of the Energies of the Universe to help make the changes you deem important. The energetic release you throw off is healthy for you and causes the physiological release of your body's chemicals to the mental stimulus of the meditation helping you to heal. You cannot harm any if you adhere to the Rede of "Harm None and Do What You Will" If you don't …the law of triples applies…it comes back to you! 3x over! Once it is out in the Realms of the Astral Plane it will be heard and used to help create changes and healings. How outraged are you? That is the strength of the power that will return for Justice. Your Magick Music weaves the Worlds.

Are you angry? Hurt? <u>All</u> anger comes from hurt—self-preservation. Do you want Justice? What is the Wound? The injustice perpetrated against you? Admit the hurt <u>and</u> what you'd really like to do or have done—what would be Justice!!??!!? Listen to yourself; hear what you are saying to you. <u>Your feelings</u> if in purple <u>are</u> <u>justified</u>. Always preface these releases of feelings with the Rede saying, "I wish harm to none, through Justice Deities may this be done." Then spout off everything you'd <u>like</u> to see done. This will cause the physiological reaction in your Body, Soul, Spirit to release anger and heal hurt in you. You are not above violence, nor "too good" for that—but keep it in meditation and release your emotions.

Fahaltryn

Violet Brow   **Merging**
Staff/Lesson Learned   **Is=Isolation**
                                                   Realignment

Truth be Known True Colors be Shown, Waiting for Change,
Transition, Gratitude Homeward

You have learned so many things. Some seem to be opposites and now you must readjust your thinking, your position and perhaps accept that there might be a better way than what you understood at first; when the Journey began.

Be Grateful that you can change, grow and learn; that you can see the omens and signs and read their meanings. Let your vision clear as the emotional tides calm. You have traveled far, whatever made you begin your Journey has been affected by you and your work—be grateful, thank then realign your beliefs according to what you have learned.

Sometimes when in Violet you'll feel that you should not relinquish your goal or the way that you think no matter what. At other times dreams and fantasies will constantly be replacing reality in your mind; changing with your mood. Seek balance.

You are free to go home—perhaps not back to where you departed from but a truer, safer home. Do you recognize the landmarks the little signs of the times and subtle hints? Through your own assisted efforts, you have gathered and fought for hard won lessons and deeply revealed Universal Truths about Honor, Love, Fairness, Acceptance, and Contracts—Regal Rights, and Forever Relationships—Timing, Boundaries, Strength, power releases and Flexibility; and now it is all merging to bring about alchemy—metaphysical changes within you and without in your life's circumstance.

The Emotional claws retract and Forgiveness, allowing another their unique Human journey, turns the raging seas to waters as smooth as glass. Forgiveness does not Excuse hurtful behavior, condone it or not feel hurt by it (Harm None always stands) but realizes the other's trauma and trials and acknowledges and allows that the other has faltered and failed at that juncture. How do you (I) like me now? Safe Voyage Home— Wanderer.

Cal%a

Pink Crown/Head   **Mystery**
Self Above Time   **Ur=Strength**
                                                      Sovereignty

Dignity, Regalness, Self-Sufficient, Mistress, Put on Your Crown, Establish Own Realm

Mysterious alchemy of Regal Sovereignty where all else falls away—true self emerges, is the crown of the Pink Realm. No Shame or Blame is cast on self or others, but a deep realization of the Divine Dignity and the truth of the Journey—never ending. The attainment of true personality balanced with real Honor. Gentle Strength—Mighty Gentleness, Self Sufficiency and Self-Direction. All the work you've done gives you the strength to take full and right responsibility for all actions, reactions, successes, failures, and stagnations. Take control by rising above time and releasing control to the higher deep-inner self—the Sacred Self. For the Love of One and the Good of All.

Sometimes when in Pink you will feel unable to accomplish your own life by yourself and at other times the fear of not being allowed self-determination will push you to be tyrannical. Seek balance.

Drawing without guilt from the fact that "I am"—knowing and using all the qualities designed into this/your life. The Primal Regal Sacred Strength of your own Realm. Establish it. Show it forth with Love, Joy and Comfort— knowing always, that allowing others to be sovereign is the highest point of sovereignty. All the things you expect people and spirits to give to you; are you giving those same things? Are you deferring to someone else even when there is no need to do so? In pink, the

Real You who has been hidden inside steps forward and claims life and Sovereign self-determination.

It is your right, privilege, responsibility, Comfort and Joy to be you. Are you ready to be?

Moon Day

White Over All   **Magick**
Moonlight   **Wyrd=Destiny**
                                                      Openness, Still Point

All things are Possible, See the Magick, Stop

Universal Truths Exist. If you have aligned with Universal Truths; Honor, Justice, Acceptance, Comfort, Joy, Creation, Strength, Sovereign Self-Determination; then the Sacred, Magickal Universe will align with you.

Those things you have wanted and worked for (if they will harm none) are arriving. Stop and be still, strain and struggle no more—believe in yourself and watch the magick happening all around you. This is the Cosmic, Karmic (not to mention sometimes Comic!) Response. If you are in white—it's like Moonlight or the gentle stillness of the moment you realize it is snowing. Life has meaning; you have meaning and you are living a Meaningful Life.

Sometimes when in white you may have the deep feeling of longing to belong, to be a part of something. At other times there may be a great fear of being swallowed up and losing Personal Identity. Seek balance. This is a good time to do a Passport.

Step back, observe—look at the changes the Magickal Universe is working. Can you see? Do you feel still? You are spiraling to a new level—a new dimension is opening for you. Are you clear about what you have intended? Know that it would not have happened except for your efforts. The Universal Principals and you are in alignment and are working together.

Are you in accord with Love? Read your journal—watch the magick; listen to the messages of your new Journey Path calling you. Where are you going, Seeker? "Be willing to seek find open and use." and now be still...

Activate

Body ~ Soul~ Spirit all interconnect and integrate.

You have Journeyed thus far, my Dear Hearted Friend.........

Are you ready now to Activate?

The Releasing Meditations follow:

Brymn
Gray

Toxins
Flu

Go to the dismal Swamp of Muzzy in Brymn. Instead of going through the Water Fall cave to Journey onward, there will be a small bridge; cross it and follow the path through the darkening swamp. Find the gray stone cottage as your pathway becomes completely fogged over and your direction confused and unclear. Hear the door creak as you enter.

You are overwhelmed, take refuge and hide yourself away here. Look around... see that the fire is simply smoldering, smoking with very little heat or flame, isn't that much the way you feel? See the cloak, fuzzy-soft and gray lying across the chair, which faces the fireplace. As you pick it up, think about why you feel the way you do...the wound...take your time and honestly identify your deep woundedness. Sit down, wrap up in the cloak and write the reason for your malaise in the little journal book there... no need to do anything about it. Write it down now so later you will not be able to deceive yourself. When in Muzzy this is the real wound surfacing. Wrap up in the cloak, identify the deep cause, write it down then set it aside and hide away... in the gray deep-swamp cottage... rest deeply... close your eyes... retreat into the grayness...admit that there is too much chaos now to deal with this issue in any way... too much Confusion.

When you are done completely close down the scene with the swirls of silvery gray mists and end your session. Take your time coming back; be sure to write the cause in your Journal

Dalwynara
Black

Go to the Black Glass Mountains and the Dalwynara Castle of Mirrors. Enter, this huge black castle carved into the slope of the mountain. It is fully furnished with mirrors of all shapes and sizes lining most of the walls... a castle of mirrors. There is a roaring fire in the fireplace and, although no people are to be found, as you begin to search through the beautiful halls and chambers, there seems to be someone watching you, stalking you— a shadow that is never quite really there but always present in your life; haunting the halls. It is the symbol of all you find annoying, aggravating and unacceptable in others. All of those things and in particular the very things that have been hurting and irritating the most just lately...all of them! The more you think about it, the more you feel your anger rise. They can't be trusted! I don't like them! So infuriated now are you that you turn on It, this Shadow....Now...Begin to chase after it. Down one passage, across this chamber, out the doorway, up the hall...the chase is difficult and confusing because of all the myriad reflections. Is it the real culprit? Until there! Finally, you come face to face with the fiend! This treacherous Shadow! But wait! It moves as you move...and stops when you stop... You realize it is yet another Mirror that you see...yourself revealed...and the Curse cures. It has been an illusive illusion that you have been chasing; and knowing the Shadow is a part of you as well as all those you find distasteful and unacceptable is sobering.

Speak your sharp curse! At that moment, all the Mirrors begin to shatter...one by one, dozens at a time...smashing, crashing glass. The noise reverberates through you like a shock wave... this shock that you too have faults; the very ones that you have complained about in others. Keep going; know that you are shattering the mirrors. The excess of energy this releases is grounded away down your legs and out your feet and into the Black Glass stone of the Mountains; freeing you to Journey onward uninhibited by the illusions of the Mirrors and now with a Sure Direction.

When you are done completely close down the scene with the swirls of silvery gray mists and end your session. Take your time coming back; write in your journal and go for a walk.

aMaun   Stability
Amber/Brown   Flexibility

Go to the Tower of Records in the aMaun Realm. The gentle hills roll on to meet the horizon. See a Celtic Round Tower rising before you. It's dark brown stonework heavy and sure; it's amber glass windows inviting. Next to it is a shorter square-shaped vault of Archives. Search, find the door you need.........

As you enter, the reality shifts and you find yourself in a huge library filled with all the records of the Universe, everything you agreed upon in the before time is here so that you may check on your progress at any time...you have the Regal Right to know! Here is the Collective Unconsciousness of the Universe. Things may be written in archetypal symbols so be aware of the flutters and don't try to analyze. Ask the Ancient aMaun Guardian of the Records for Your Book... if you cannot read the writing the Librarian will translate for you. Seat yourself on the small sofa in front of the copper-domed fireplace. There is a pot of hot tea waiting for you; enjoy it. Look at Your Book; note its color and decoration... Title? Flip through the pages until you find the right page; you will know when you find it. Ask to be shown what it is you are questioning...wondering about... but remember, maybe you don't really want to know...When you do access what is written in your Book, try to acknowledge and accept it, it will give you the surety and flexibility to bend the knee to contracted agreements and stay Stable.

When you are done, completely close down the entire scene with the swirls of silvery gray mists; end your session. Take your time coming back; when done write what you learned in your Journey book and try to be very accurate, don't add in your own wishes or pre-conceived thoughts on the subject; that's why you sought out the Higher Consciousness. Your stay in aMaun will help you to stay stable and honorable through being flexible.

Tolus   Challenge
Burgundy   Make a Stand
                                                  Attack/be Attacked

Go to the Plains of Toorn, with your Battle Hammer in hand...this is War! See the encampment of your troops in the shelter of the slope beneath the Battle Plain. Here there are thickets and thorns, brush and brambles. Gather your strength, your allies, your honor and your power. Be ready to face the Enemy for they are advancing to attack you on the Battlefield. Go into your command tent and make a plan— declare your war. There are some things worth fighting for; is this one of them? Be honest and Honorable. If so, strategize with your allies and comrades...who will stand with you? Do you know? Don't rush...listen to your allies...perhaps, at this point, you may see a different way; but, if not, plan your offense and defense here and now.

As you come out of the tent, survey your army...these are your clan...you are their Regal Lord/Lady and they respect you and look to you for leadership and wisdom. Remember the confrontation...who/what is the enemy? What is the hurt and dishonor? In the distance, begin to hear their battle drums and the stomping, angry troops and horses as they rage their hatred towards you. The air is tense with emotion. They are coming. You have no choice in the matter any longer; they have brought the battle to you. Mount your horse... feel it's strength and power beneath your thighs. Draw your weapon. Wait...ready... Now! Give the command to Charge! Fight fiercely! Slashing, smashing as harshly and with as much savagery as you need to use, let out all your anger, hurt, aggression, and sorrow! Vent it upon the enemy! All of them or perhaps it is with just one of them that you fight. Here- you win. Remember that; so keep on, keep on and keep on.........until you do.

As the clash and fray lessen and fade, as the smoke and dust settle, see that your army is victorious. Count the cost. Who has fallen? Who has lost? Now, look down amongst the trailing thorns and brambles. Find the rose and know you have maintained honor through this Confrontation.

When you are done completely close down the scene with the swirls of silvery gray mists and end your session. Take your time coming back; write in your journal and, holding your "sword" in your hand, be grateful that no one will ever be willfully abused by you.

Oban
Red

Life Force
Sexual Energy
Physical Discipline

Go to the Ancient Ochan forest in Oban's Realm. See the enormous, dark trees with the ornate houses built into the hollows and branches. There are bridges and walkways winding around the trunks like serpents and the gnarled roots weave their patterns throughout the forest floor. See yourself sitting with Oban on an Ochan balcony, watching one of the Daeg Fires below; the flames are so hot and fierce that they seem on the verge of leaping out of their place and destroying the entire Ancient forest. Oban asks you if you have kept up with the Ritual of Movement reminding that we all need it to stay disciplined and vital. "Like the Daeg Fire", he explains, "it takes discipline to remain there, where it is fed, cared for and can burn fiercely but with constancy. It could just as easily escape, burn out of control, ferociously devouring our forest and all of us in its path. Then, when exhausted, die. What kind of purpose would that serve?" He asks if you have any new plans and you explain what they are.........he asks you why? To help you define and refine your motives...be honest. Why?......

The bell rings for the Ritual of Movement. You all go down to the pavilion where the Daeg Fire burns in towering flames. Feel yourself moving, stretching, and working through the Ritual. Then, slowly begin dancing to the Thunder Drums' insistent pulse. Let yourself get caught in the rhythm. Then the eerie droning, evocative sound of the Horn Pipes takes you under its spell. Move! Dance! With sexual urgency feel the Life Force begin to surge through your pelvis moving up through your body with Living Fire. Your drive and ambition ignite, as you leap like the flames! Dance with the Fire with no thought of inhibition! Gyrate and Rejuvenate and Create!

When you are done completely close down the scene with the swirls of silvery gray mists and end your session. Take your time coming back; when done take time to watch a flame and be grateful for discipline... Dance!

Zaphir   Desires
Orange   Vocation

Go to the Desert Dwellings of Owna. Feel the warmth and dryness of the air, see the rusty rocks and high mesas. Zaphir is working in clay as she waits for you to arrive. She hands you a large lump of clay and asks you what it is you want to make. Who are you ready to be? Make something...pound the clay and use all the will and power and strength you can to make the clay into the image of what you would like to see occur in your life. Check your motive again. (from the Red Realm) and now check your intent. What do you intend to do with what you are calling forth? Be very honest for if you are not truly honorably honest now what you manifest may be distorted and even harmful. Put your clay piece in the kiln, close the door...Zaphir will give you a wand to direct your Life force into the piece in the kiln. The heat rises and the energy vibrates from deep within your belly...you are calling forth your deepest self. Feel the super energy charge pass along out of you, then out through the Wand...wait...send your intentions out through your Wand...for what in this Life do you wait? Answer this important question...now open the oven...what is there? Are you ready for this new existence in your life that you have just called forth in to being? Are you ready to be with new Purpose?

When done completely close down the scene with the swirls of silvery mists and end the session. Take your time coming back...hold your wand.

Delania   Fears
Peach   self Defense

Go to Delania's charming and disarming rose covered cottage where you will be protected, defended and have the good fortune to have your immunity strengthened. See the peach roses and the jasmine blossoms climbing, clinging and cascading along the white picket fence and the lattice archway. Everything seems so quaint and innocent but for some reason you feel uneasy in the quiet...could it be this easy? "No." you think, "something will get me...I must be on my guard...always ready to find a way to take care of "me", to get what I need and want because no one will be there for me. I know how they are...can't trust them...they'll disappoint me...just when I think I can have everything I want it will be snatched away." As you wander through he wonderful rooms, see how calm and peaceful life could be if you could stop imagining that something is waiting to get you; if you could stop thinking that the quiet is a threat to who you are; preferring the storm because it proves you are strong and exciting. A big orange cat stretches in the sunshine. You hear him purr to you "no one ever gets everything they want and if you keep making others give you what you want...you will miss out on the wonderful gifts that they would give you of their own accord and the delight of manifesting your wants, needs and desires by your own power. Fear keeps you manipulating and pride keeps you fighting even when there is no cause."

Look in the mirror; see the heavy chain belt around your waist. As a symbol of releasing yourself from this pattern of manipulation and fear take it off and put it away. Find an article of adornment in the cottage that speaks encouragement to you and put it on to remind you that life is hard and you cannot escape hardship but there is so much to enjoy so have Courage!

When done close down the scene completely with the swirls of silvery gray mists and end your session. Take your time coming back, write in your Journal and use adornment!

Courtheon
Yellow

Expanding Awareness
New Thoughts

Go to Courtheon—the Heart of the government of all Hammeril. As you arrive, see the wonderful sea-washed village on the East coast with its friendly people and busy shops. Walk along the cobble stoned streets aglow in the bright sunshine until you come to the bright cream- colored domed building of the Courtheon. Push open the heavy carved wooden double doors. There is Arom the rotund and happy Chancellor and he tells you how glad they all are that you have arrived. "It is time to match your outer actions to those inner beliefs which have been dawning within you." He explains as he leads you to the Chair Room where you meet the Regal Lord/Lady. Your eyes spark intense recognition...it's been too long in coming; this meeting of Soul Mates —each possessing the qualities the other needs and desires. That you may be lacking something and needing to grow or change and that someone else could help complete you is irritating and even angers both of you. And although you long for acceptance by the Regal one you fear rejection more—you both do. "It is time to put down your box!" Arom says and hands you an ornate delightfully carved golden box..." when you are ready, and this is the heart of the reason for your Journey, you will be able to take all that you think you know, put it in this box, and set it aside, only then will you each be free to learn anything new and become enlightened." Your stomach tightens as you receive the box from his hands and look across at the Regal One...Are you ready to accept this new thought and Expand your Boundaries? Reach into your pocket; find there a symbol of the Change you need to make and place it in the Golden Box. Arom will place it safely on the shelf. See your other self, (soul mate, Lord/Lady, Yin/Yang) do the same. Understand this is an agreement to be open to changes and lessons.

When you are done close down the scene completely with the swirls of silvery gray mists and end your session. Take your time coming back; write in your Journal and place your box in a visible place of honor.

Jaedn
Lime

Manifest
Come Forth!

Go to the Well of Desire in Jaedn where all the beautiful stone buildings are moss covered and ivy hung. As your friends and guides rush out to meet you, feel very much at home in this wonderful village...perhaps there are old friends there whom you haven't seen in a while. Feel the recognition. You tell them you need to go to the well and one of them steps forward to escort you as the others take their leave to go on about their lives. Through the busy streets, past the shops and then out the narrow back alley, you go. Then, with effort, push on, up the steep rocky slope to the stone well house. Smell the musty dampness as you enter the arched doorway. The walls of this little building are dripping and trickling with springlets and lush with the green growth of mosses, ivies and vines. Torchlight flickers and adds to the mystery..."Make your Wish" your friend smiles...What is it you have been striving for on your Journey, walking towards, working out? Make your wish now and be very specific. Drop the bucket into the deep well. Hear the splash as it hits the water below; wait as it fills and sinks deep into the Well of Desire. Now pull...pull...begin to haul on the rope to retrieve the bucket. As you do, your ribs and chest ache... and there it is... set the bucket of water on the edge of the well...reach your hand into the cold, cold, water... what is the symbol you have been given? Pull it out. Surprised? You will be given that which you have really been doing the work for on your Journey. Your friend will help you to understand the meaning; be still and listen carefully; remembering that you must always be truthful with yourself and the Otherworld guides and energies and not try to get your own way without balancing it with how it might effect others. Thank your friend. Splash some cold water from the bucket on your face to refresh you and your motives and drink some from your cupped hand to help cool your striving and frustrations.

When done, close down the scene completely with the swirls of silvery gray mists and end your session. Take your time coming back, write in your Journal and add a stone to your fountain.

Catherine L. Avizinis

Tesque   Healing
Green   Abundance

Go to the Gardens in Tesque's Realm where you will be engulfed by the abundance of green growing healing herbs, and healing relationships. Perhaps you need some tea or a poultice or warm oil treatment designed for your special healing. The Chimere; an herbal hospital with harps, incense, fresh air and sunshine, is a place of comfort and joy despite the illness, pain or heartache. The attendants approach you; tell them where you hurt, what you need, ask to be taken care of and let them help. Feel the warm green oil saturating your wounded ness, smell the herbs, taste the tea and drink it fully.

This is the place where your wounds are acknowledged and validated... feel the wonderful healing as they allow you to be you and you understand that the best healing is to accept others for who they are and not expecting them to be you...just love them for who they are and not for who you wish they could be to suit your ways and beliefs. Tesque takes you for a walk out through the rolling hills of every herb and flower you can imagine. Smell the life and see how all the plants just grow to their best beauty without condemning each other or faulting differences. "Allow the paints to heal your" she says..." they will take your grief if you let them." Now lift up your arms like a tree and allow that other person to be...without your restriction or condemnations... if you can do this you will feel the surge of healing, the breath of life and truly you will Love!

Jy   Play
Aqua   Be cared for

Go to the seaside Pavilion on Isle Vaide. Golden sands shimmer in the sunshine; the frothy waves rush in and play then sweep back out again as you stroll along the beach so happy to see the bright blue-green crystal waters of life. Feel the warmth of the sun ease away the ache of burdens from your shoulders, walk through the waters... plough your legs along... skip along the sands... dance with the waves! Now run...twirl... play... and feel the laughter begin to bubble up and let it giggle out of you in a squeal and shout! Yell your release into the wind! Shout out, "I need play time! And I'm taking it!"... Without it we fizzle out and are in danger of loosing happiness. You need to ask to be pampered...There! See that glorious silky tent Pavilion up ahead? Go there and ask whom ever you find for a fine luxurious oil massage. In this brightly colored tent, lounging on the soft pillows, here is a gift for you and you deserve it. The comfort level is just right; the temperature is perfect. Feel yourself receiving the wonderful gift of being touched; focus on the warm oil being massaged into each part of your body... one at a time... slowly, especially the neck and shoulders. Don't rush. The Jy oil is poured on and soaks into your body as all the "stored" duty /responsibility, guilt and resentment are worked out of your muscles and nerves. Let this release move slowly and purposefully; slowly and purposefully. In your deep relaxation you faintly hear the voice of Jy, who has stopped in to check on you. She says, "Rest on, Young One, Rest on".

Then, when you are done, thank your caregiver for what you have received and venture out to play some more in the waves. Look! Up ahead in the waters! A bottle is washing up on shore! How exciting! Run! Catch it! There is a message inside. Take out the paper...and read it...believe it...remember it. All of this fun and remember ... No Guilt!

When done, close down the scene completely with the swirls of silvery gray mists and end your session. Take your time coming back; write in your Journal especially note the Message in the Bottle.

Kriel   Self Worth

Blue   Measure up

Go to Kriel's Realm of ice and snow where the clan lodges are big and warm, all are welcome and the feasts are endless. Begin trudging up the last ice bridge as the village comes into view. Feel the sharp cold and see the mists of your breath in the frosty air. Ahead are the log long houses with dragonheads on the crossed bargeboards...their colors all the brighter against of the stark whiteness of the snow. In the harshness of this reality, joy soars that you are so welcomed here and not left out in the cold to fend for yourself...shared meagerness becomes abundance. Gleaming, clear crystals are lying all about and it is hard to tell which are ice crystals and which are stone! Prismatic reflections sparkle and it is truly thrilling to have arrived right on time...

As you enter the clan house, you feel a deep sameness connecting you with all who are gathered there and yet all of you know that each is unique...the joy of unique self worth and belonging at the same time... Here you know truly that you don't have to give up self in order to fit in, but are appreciated for what you can offer...take time to remember this...take a moment to drink in this joy. The eldest clan Mother takes your arm as she walks you to the center of the room. "It is your turn—" she smiles and winks at you. "It's my turn to be_____!" you declare. What a joy...to declare for whatever you think it is now time...anything... and to know that it is time for it to be addressed. You are applauded...and then it is someone else's turn...this goes on and on. One of your Clan Cousins offers to walk with you to the Crystal River of Time to be certain that the timing is right...that you're not too early and will end up waiting in disappointment and not too late and will have missed the opportunity to find your happiness. See the two of you trudging out through the snows and arriving at the River's edge. The icy waters bubble and sing as they splash along down the side of the slope...life is in the ice crystal...such a small thing to find...take out your old time piece and smash it in order to break any bond it might have to you and let it go down the river. Now, reach in through the ice crystals and rock crystals and find your new timepiece...more refined each time you visit the Blue Realm...To know that I am worth this... I am worth the air I breathe, the Space I take up and the Food I eat. Thank your clan cousin. I am worth being noticed, heard and believed. I am worthy! What a Joy!

When done, completely close down the scene with the swirls of silvery gray mists and end your session. Take your time coming back, write in your Journal and watch for timing. Commune with your crystals.

Daemus   Imagine
Indigo   Articulate

Go to the Castle of the Night Sky where tales are told, wit and laughter ring through the halls and mystical enchantments flow empowered by imagination and whimsy. As you approach, you suddenly realize that this dark indigo castle is not on a high hilltop as it appears to be but floats out in the starry expanse of the heavens and to reach it you must use your imagination...fly? how? a bird? a wisp of smoke? Any way you choose. Up through the clouds—the diamond stars twinkling, the mauve clouds seeping through the inky blackness...magick is afoot! Wizards and Mages, Seers and Sorceresses...friends and family...hear the laughter. The sharing of stories continues on and on into the night...not all are humorous...some tell a sad and tragic tale, but all are welcome to tell and are equally heard and applauded.

Do you need to ask advice? Is someone not hearing what you've been saying...even though you've been saying it over and over and over again? Tell on them here and now. Take your time and speak freely. Tell on them! Daemus asks, "Are you trying to work at it in order to fix and heal it or just to be right, to be heard?" Be honest; listen to the advice and suggestions of all the others gathered there. Then be free to use your wonderful imagination to come up with a new way to say the same old thing...tell it in a new way knowing that your thoughts are the powers, the alchemy, for change...this is your spell work. Daemus puts his robed arm across your shoulders and whispers in your ear, "*Your* willfully chosen words have the primal powers of the *Universe...*do not take them lightly" and he then gives you a special word to say or a phrase... hear it...

This is for your key power in this issue—*Thank Daemus* and the others for their help. *Now* speak...tell... hear the new way you need to tell of your boundaries, fears, wants, needs, desires and opinions. *Use* your *Magickal Word* from *Daemus* to unlock these words when you are back in *Reality* and to empower your words with *Imagination!*

When done close down the scene completely with the swirls of silvery gray mists and end your session. *Take* your time coming back; write in your *Journal* and then speak your words outloud!

Pryll   Emotions
Purple   All Claires

Go to the deep purple, high cliffs of Justice near Pryll's castle. A storm is raging there with smashing waves, angry thunder, firecracks of lightning! Scream out for justice! Below you see the ocean violently beating against the rocks and feel your passions exploding. You have fought for hard won acquisitions and made personal progress and now what ever the hurt, whatever the wrong done to you...your feelings are justified...as the storm rages within and without around about you call for your assailant to appear your adversary and all others you would like to be present...Accuse...Rage!...make your case and scream out what you feel would be justice. You are the witness, judge and jury and executioner...keep crying out and declaring for justice for you are right! Your feelings are your own and cannot be invalidated and there is no competition here...you are unique with specific circumstances. Feel the surging power of the lightning bolts and the huge directed energy of the winds and rains. Feel the volatile releases with each boom of Thunder and strike of lightning as you exact Justice here and now!

At a distance you notice a figure robed in deep, dark purple. The strains from the harp this Mage is playing begin to fill the air, sounding over the storm. This Magick Music is haunting...and as it calms your raging-electric energy it also strangely amplifies your wishes and intentions. The music builds and builds as you become one with the waves, one with the storm and one with the music and one with Justice...release your magick powers... See yourself standing in a star stance, arms and legs stretched wide and know that you are releasing your power into the Astral Plane where it will be used to rain truer justice back down to our Earth Plane. The storm will subside. Thank the Mage and the others for helping you... your passions, feelings and intuitions are your Power!

When done, close down the scene completely with the swirls of silvery gray mists and end your session. Take your time coming back, write in your Journal and enjoy music.

Fahaltryn
Violet

Gratitude
Transition

Go to the misty Island of Fahaltryn. The hooded boatman works his oar as you silently glide over a sea as calm and smooth as glass. Violet mists join sea and sky as you land on the Island of the Sleeping Dragon—a great peace soothes your soul. You feel alone, but alone is just what you want now... Thank and pay the Boatman with the magick penny that always appears in your purse when needed, and start up the rocky slope on the long trek to the sea cottage. Find, as you go along, an unusual staff, left there just for you by your soul mate...it will have meaning and be a great encouragement and comfort to you in this alone time.

The winds pick up and the mists clear away the higher you climb. The higher you climb the more clear-headed you become and the more forgiveness and gratitude merge within you. "Truth be Known; True Colors be Shown"...whispers rhythmically in your head with each step of your climb...and you begin to understand the fullness of this phrase...Think back over the many Realms through which you have passed and the lessons you have learned...Remember why you began your Journeywork in the first place...with each step recall your great progress traveling the tangled knot work of your path. See how things have changed. Have things smoothed out in your issue? The more honorable your motives and pure your intentions the more you manifest what you want at the end...and just perhaps...what you wanted truly& deeply has manifested instead of those things you only thought you wanted. Forgiveness; allowing another to be human and frail, too. Enter the wind blown cottage clinging to the weathered rocks and wait during this time of merging, transition and realignment. In this cottage you will find a treasure of various materials that you may use to add a symbol of accomplishment to your staff. See your hands as you make this addition and remember that each person carries their own Journey Staff with marks of merit and symbols of suffering; badges of their own lessons learned. Admire your staff and feel gentle waves of gratitude wash over you. How wonderful to be homeward bound...Gratitude!

When done, close down the scene completely with the swirls of silvery gray mists and end your session. Take your time; when back write in your Journal and add a symbol to your staff.

Calya   **Sovereignty**

Pink   **Dignity**

Go to the Sacred Site in your own newly established Realm...What kind of Realm do you wish to form...what is your strength? Only you can make your Realm—it is a task for no one else. See the Standing Stones among the Pink heather and just beyond there is a Dolmen. Know that this is where you will build your castle. This is the gathering place of your clan. Enter with wonder and authority...all your friends and allies are here taking their ease and anxiously waiting for you to arrive. They greet you with cheers and embraces and you recognize the faces and the spirits and the aromas. The leadership feels awkward yet exhilarating. A song is sung and played in your honor...stop...listen...enjoy this...try to hear the words or remember the tune...then your closest friend nods and you know it is time to finally go to the back sacred hall...Make your way through the passage and into the chamber. There sitting in honor waiting for you is the Crown of your Birthright...the Regal Crown of the Realms...like a thousand pink fire lights it shimmers. Your hands feel the power surge as you lift it from its place...with great awe and humility you place it on your own head; accepting the responsibility to establish who you are, your Regal Realm and to honorably serve One and All...with wit, dignity, strength, self-sufficiency, gentleness. Thank your friend for being there for you. As you step back out through the passage and into the main hall to the cheers of your Clan; tears sting your eyes.

They allow you to pass... but not without another song! Go outside the sun is setting in pink and gold glory. Walk among the Standing Stones of the Ancients...enter the inner circle. Let the Power of Regalness floods you. Vow to always live and profess that the highest point of Sovereignty is to let another be Sovereign. Know that some of the energies of Attainment of the True Self are now yours...Sovereignty!

When done completely close down the scene with the swirls of silvery gray mists and end your session. Take your time coming back; Journal and then treat yourself!

Moon Day
White

Still Point
All is Possible

Go to the magickal Center of the Land of Hammeril, the Stillpoint in the White Realm...it is a Moon Day...an eclipse of the Sun by the Moon. The Festival, the Banners, the Musicians and people in their fete attire, bells and harnesses chingling, drums and dancing feet, horns and shouts of play, the Moon Day has arrived! See the gleaming white castle of Shune Shulee as Mythical and Mystical as anything you have ever seen. And as the Moon begins to touch the Sun, the crowd begins its reverence. Sweet melodies swell, groups of friends gather, arms linked...Scenes of the Journey Flutter past your memory... take a few moments to reflect...and you know that it is true...you have done all that is within your power to do to bring about truth, honor, justice and loving acceptance for the Love of just One and the Good of All...now as you enter White Still Point on this most Magickal of days you know the supernatural response will happen...is happening...and you are open to Destiny..."Today is the Destination of the Past", someone announces, "and we are here!" The crowd cheers and then suddenly and softly falls silent as the eclipse is made whole and you feel your old self, new self and future self all merged. The first snowflakes begin their spiraling dance...you belong to this wholeness. Thank yourself, be grateful to all and any who have helped you... you have all done well...it is Magick...All is possible...You are all One in the Stillness!

When done, completely close down the scene with the swirls of silvery gray mists and end your session. You're your time coming back, write in your Journal and after...draw spirals.

Steps for Rituals

✴ Determine Your color and do the Chapter work
✴ Gather the Materials you will Need:

- Bath Salts
- Oils/Mysts
- Robe or Fabrics in Your Color
- Crystals/Jewelry
- the Realm tool (ex. Gray-a cloak, Violet-a staff)
- Music to Enhance (Red-Brass/ very pounding
- Rhythm, Yellow-Flute or CD's that suit you.)
- Soft Lights (please be careful with candles!)
- Dimmer Light or an Enclosed lantern can be very nice.
- Your Journey-wise Workbook & Journal
- Anything else you would personally like to add.

Preparing thoughtfully prevents disruption later during your Ritual. (Note—Know the Direction Points N-S-E-W of your space). A Ritual is any set of steps we use to alert the inner self that a change is about to take place. Although not a daily requirement, Ritual will help you make more potent changes.

Assemble your tools and calm yourself. Recall your color and what it means and also what it is specifically that you are about to try to accomplish then, light your lamp.

Call in all kind and Helpful Energies to assist you and align with you. Stand facing the West.

Lift the lantern and call out.

"I am on my Journey Quest oh Wondrous Waters of the West—I call to the Ancestors to help me find my path. **Lower lantern to "path"**
I acknowledge you My Ancestral Family..."

"...and the connections which link me to you. May you bring to me understanding of myself and my powers on this part of my Journey."

"Energies Sweet, Energies Strong
Justice and Truth sing your Song
Power of the Waters, Power of the Waves
I honor the West and what Life's Mystery Gave."

Holding up your lantern, move slowly to face the North.

"I am Journeying Forth oh Nurturing North, I call to the Nature Energies to help me find my path.

Lower lantern

" I acknowledge the clockwork of the Universe and this Natural World and that I am a part of the structure and flow...may you bring to me self-worth and proper alignment on this part of my Journey."

"Energies Sweet, Energies Strong
Comfort and Joy Sing your Song
Power of Earth Plant Crystal and Stone
I honor the North and Journey not Alone."

Holding up the lantern, move slowly to the East.

"I am willing to feast oh Enlightening Winds of the East, I call to the Powers of Light and Air to help me find my path."

Lower lantern

"I acknowledge the need for releasing what I know in order that I may grasp the new things. May you bring to me change on this part of my Journey."

"Energies Sweet, Energies Strong
Change and Expansion Sings your Song
Power of Air, Power of Light
I honor the East for my wings of Flight."

Holding up the lantern, move slowly to face the South.

"I will keep on, I vow, oh Splendid Fire of the South. I call on the Transforming powers of Fire to help me find my path."

Lower the lantern

"I acknowledge the creative Life-Force and that I may use it to create harmony or hindrance. May you bring to me fiery pure motives on this part of my Journey."

"Energies Sweet, Energies Strong
Challenge and Honor Sing your Song
Power of Hammer, Wand and Flame
I honor the South with a Fire the same."

Holding up the lantern complete the circle facing West, go to the center and call out:

"Spiritual Realms I call for Protection from anything which may hinder or harm—I now Enter into the (color) Ritual of (purpose) of the Realm of _____.

Place your lantern in a safe place and myst or anoint yourself and your space with appropriate color blend and visualize yourself surrounded with the energies, or if you're doing a Ritual bath now is the time to draw it and with intent slowly scrub with the salts and then luxuriate in the waters for as long as you'd like. When done, towel off then apply the appropriate oil and do the appropriate Movement and see your space filling with the Energies. Place the tools near you and the crystals on the charkas. Now it is time for the Releasing Meditation. Try to read and visualize the meditation at the same time—after a few times you'll remember it well enough to simply do the release. Remember these Rituals and Visualizations will facilitate physiological release by employing mental stimulus—go with the flow of your emotions the flutter of image—your first thoughts are the most telling so don't try to figure anything out just watch the "film." And if your mind takes you in another direction go with that, too. After all you're seeking deep knowledge—if you access something be proud of yourself, it could be an important piece to your puzzle quest. Sometimes you may have trouble "seeing"; don't worry, just keep going and feel the perception of the words you are reading.

(*Note—There are times when our puzzle is just too traumatic to try to put it back together on our own. Please; many highly trained, beautifully compassionate doctors and therapists are available Journey-wise is not meant as a substitute for Professional assistance—never try to live alone. If you are overly distraught, sad, suicidal, afraid or lonely—tell someone.)

After you close down the meditation give yourself time to Return, Rest and Reflect, before making your Journal Entry.

Then close down the entire circle of energy you have created. Safe Passage.

Sample Ritual Bath

Make Entries in your Journey Book like this:

Date: Jan. 27, 03

_____Yellow_____ Ritual of Expansion of the Realm of Matching.

Courtheon

My Issue: <u>I feel a slight discontent, something new is coming.</u>

I gather to me:
>Courtheon Bath Salts, Oils, Myst
>a Golden Towel and Yellow Robe and Scarf
>Sulfur Crystals
>a Gold Necklace and Armband with Sunbursts
>a Carved Yellow Box w/ Sun faces
>Native American Flute Music CD
>a Sunburst Votive Lantern w/ Lemon Candle
>a Pen and Yellow Paper

Start music to continuous play and light the lantern and call in the Directions ending with "I call on Spirit Realms to protect me from anything which may hinder or harm. I now enter into the Yellow Ritual of Expansion of the Realm of Matching." Set the lantern in a safe place and draw a hot bath. Soak then with purpose, acknowledging the discontent and the changes you feel coming. Gently scrub with your Courtheon Salts and rinse. Relax, review your issue, do some deep relaxation breathing in which you feel and visualize Yellow Energies Flowing in, out, around and through your entire being. Spend as long as you'd like on that step! Decide to Journey. Towel off and apply oil/myst all over especially to the yellow charka (never to mucus membranes or irritated or sensitive skin) and put on jewelry. Next, do the "Thru the Gate Exercise."

#2 Yellow—Thru the Gate...make the decision to Journey. Enter into participation in your <u>own</u> <u>life</u>. Put down your Box, Slowly drop over and then roll the spine up: knees flexed, elbows rounded up to the ceiling, pelvis forward, head down until all the way up. Put on your robe and scarf (or go sky clad naked). Next lay on the floor or bed within your circle, feet to center, head to East and place the Crystals on the solar plexus and near head/eyes, and perform meditation. Go behind the waterfall, down the tunnel and out into the brightest light where you find your Golden Horse all dressed in yellow/gold. Ride to the village of Hammeril to the East and proceed to the Government buildings of the Courtheon. Complete the Meditation from the Courtheon Meditation pages.

When you have closed down the scene and are back in your space, write down on the paper those things you feel are to changing and put them in your Box. Ceremoniously lift it high above your head and speak your phrase—"I put down my box and Open!" Now, put it slowly down. With this Ritual step you are telling the Multidimensional One and All that you truly desire to change these things. Give yourself some quiet time to simply enjoy your space. To truly be open means to try not to plan what <u>you</u> think should happen. Believe that there could be more possibilities than you can comprehend right now. Feel yourself absorbing all the Golden Yellow Light you can from this wonderful Energy Transducer you have created.

When you are done—lift the lantern to the Directions in turn in reverse—to the South, East, North, West, and Center.

"I thank and bless for your help given anew. May I in turn share my Life Fire, Enlightenment, Nurturing Power and Protection with you."

Then as you lift the lantern high, send any remaining Yellow energy of your Ritual out into the Astral Plane to be added to the abundance.

"Merry meet Merry Part and Merry we'll meet again."

Visualize the vanishing of your circle and all those who came to help you. Mentally close the door and end the Ritual. You do not want any "leaking" of energies to happen. This is very important. Much damage and confusion can occur if you are not Responsible enough for your actions to Keep the Worlds Separate. It is your Honorable Duty.

Clean up when ready. Put your tool, in this case, your BOX in a visible place of honor.

Being "in" a color or Realm means that your Unique Journey Path has led you to this place at this time and given You the Enlightened Energies and power abilities to Balance these particulars.

When in a color you need to do the works of that color and only that color. To put another Realms work into your life at this time is pure Folly! You have enough to accomplish with your stay in your Color-Coded Realm Message for the day or until it changes.

Each time you enter into a particular Realm you will be working on different pieces of your life's Puzzle Map so that you will have slightly different answers and specifics available to you to gain insight into the "why's" of your core beliefs and the "How to's" of breaking down patterns and beliefs which no longer serve your health, happiness wholeness or honor and the "What's next's" of building the life Realm You would truly like to live.

Brymn

Gray   Ritual for Retreat

Rosemary Basil Myrrh Mint

Feeling Overwhelmed	Nervous Exhaustion
Sleep/Insomnia	Respiratory aid
Toxins	Restless Legs
Colds/Flu	Restless Thoughts
Cellulite	Memory/Mental Fatigue
Aches and Pains	Stimulate Body Energies
Head Congestion	Nausea
Infections/Wounds	Digestive aid
Cleanses Breath	Headaches
Body Normalizer	Mouth Sores

Each time you're in Muzzy honestly name the wound and you'll be able to deal with it another day. Confusion helps find the real problem.

Tool: Cloak*   Rune: Hagal=chaos   Realm Muzzy

Stones: Anything plain solid and gray (solid beach stone)

Placed: Close to Body all over. Head in North West.

Phrase: "J retreat, J rest, J hide"

Movement: None! Or Salutation #3

Music: none or anything.

Special Suggestions:

Remember when visiting in Muzzy you can't do anything, so enjoy retreating! It's the best thing right now. Add a heating pad for more comfort or place the stones in hot water to warm them first. Wrap that cozy cloak* around you and disappear. You'll know you're in Muzzy when you reach the Brymn Waterfall but just don't want to go through! Don't. Cross the stepping stones, follow the path—it will be very soggy and foggy. Find the cozy cottage, name the pain and wrap up in your cloak of invisibility, that's all you can do and it's enough.

Dalwynara

Black   Ritual of Sacred Path

Vetiver Nutmeg Cinnamon

Feeling Scattered	Lack Direction
Prevents Infections	Calmings
Cuts and Scrapes	Helps Focus and Ground
Digestion	Feeling Overwhelmed
Diarrhea	Trauma

Each time you're in Dalwynara, a new piece of your Journey Map is revealed and the fear or dismay over an illusive shadow an illusive shadow is exposed and shattered. The scary thing, which is always there, like your shadow.

Tool: Mirrors   Rune: Rad=journey   Realm of Mirrors

Stones: onyx, hematite, tektite, magnetics

Placed: at feet and top of head. Head in North East.

Phrase: "Shatter these illusions!"

Movement: toe/heel, heel/toe Begin Walking #1

Music: flutes, pipe organ, drums, bowed glass

Special Suggestions:

Think of the past 24 hours. Can you hear yourself complaining about someone else's behavior? That's your shadow—you do that same thing and you find it unacceptable in yourself as well. It needs to have light shone upon it; face it, deal with it your path **is** Sacred; embrace your shadows!

A Black-backed Scrying Mirror* or Crystal Ball* can help you to see more clearly when you face yourself. Magnetic therapies help to balance. Pictures or Replicas of Castles help to remind us of the many fascinating facets, towers and

133

spires, within our own complex nature as well as the fractured flaws, dungeons and darkened rooms. Each time you are in black try to go a different direction when you enter the Castle, Chasing down all your shadows and just Exploring. Try this: dim the lights then stare into the mirror trying to focus each eye at itself. This balances magnetic fields. Your shadow pieces are necessary to the fullness of your character.

aMaun
Brown   Ritual of Acknowledging

Amber Frankincense Vanilla

Warming	Relax Tightness
Tonic	Eases Recollections
Nerve Soother	Knee Pains
Tendons	Sprains
Antiseptic	Sedative
Spiritual Heightening	Wounds
Uterine Tonic	Skin Rejuvenation

Each time you go to the Tower of Records you may ask for information on contracted agreements or events in your life or past lives. The answers may be in symbols (as when you are dreaming for one is not usually able to read in dreams) and you will more easily acknowledge another's authority over you.

Tool: Tower of Records   Rune: Odal=security   Realm of Meanings

Stones: amber, brown jasper, agate, tiger's eye, petrified wood

Placed: at knees and crown of head. Head to East.

Phrase: "I Want (Need) to Know."

Movement: Flying Horse # 14

Music: Flutes, reeds, oboe

Special Suggestions:

Going deep into the Self can reveal our life's deep meanings—when we access these records the information can be life changing. Remember Everything has meaning and Honor gives meaning to everything—live a Life full of Meaning.

Books* are Towers of Records—so many from which to learn. Learn from others, Wisdom and gather your favorites around you like friends. Pictures or replicas of Celtic Towers help us to connect this Earth Plane with the other

Dimensions. Your Inner-, Outer-, and Other-World connectios. You had a plan when you entered—access it and follow it—that's why you are here.

Tolus

Burgundy   Ritual of Battle

Cedarwood Patchouli Orange Cardamom

Disease Discourager	Respiration
Nourishing	Circulation
Strengthening	Digestion
Refreshing	Fatigue
Skin Rejuvenation	Weight Loss
Aphrodisiac	Dispel Depression
Releasing	Rejuvenator

Each time you are in Burgundy your Mettle is tested. Can you stand and fight for a just cause if you need to do so? And do it with honor? Break down tyrants, strategize and battle; confrontations and fierceness.

Tool: Battle Hammer   Rune: Thorn=destruction   Realm of Mettle

Stones: garnet, bloodstone, ironstone, jaspers

Placed: on thighs and shoulders with head to the South West.

Phrase: "Charge! Charge! Charge! Charge!"

Movement: Battle #14, Attitude #11

Music: Pipes and Drums

Special Suggestions:

Know the enemy and know your allies, don't fight blindly. Make a plan, Make a stand. Then vent upon the enemy. When in Burgundy it is time to confront and really break down an old pattern—you may not 'win' but at least it's a change; go from there.

Gather to you your Sword or Battle Hammer—something to symbolize to you a warrior's weapon; plastic sword or a letter opener or carpenters hammer will do. These are reminders that we all must stand up for ourselves to others—Justice, Truth, Comfort and Joy. These are actions of love. Smash Your Fears!

Smash your enemies! Smash the unjust policies! We are <u>all</u> afraid. The reality of holding even the symbol of a weapon will keep you mindful of the horrors of actually inflicting pain or hurt on anyone. The Meditation will help you release those chemicals that build up because we can't and shouldn't use physical force or violence to solve our problems. Let your skillful, honorable words win your victories. Smash in meditation only!!!

Oban

Red   Ritual of Fire

Rosewood Black Pepper Basil

Eases Vomiting/Diarrhea   Strengthens Resolve
Feeds Cell Structure   Increases Sexuality
Stimulates Body's Energies   Frees Creativity
Eases Inhibitions   Purifies Air
Fatigue   Weight Loss
Aphrodisiac   Stamina

Each time you enter Red you need to re-fire your physical disciplines, exercise, eating—and look at your Motivation. Harm none with your fire.

Tool: Fire* Rune: Daeg=immediacy   Realm of Movement

Stones: Ruby, Red jasper, Bloodstone

Placed: at genitals, pelvis, and chest. Heat to South

Phrase: 'Burn! Fires, Burn.'

Movement: Hip rotations—Attitudes #11

Music: Horns and Drums.

Special Suggestions: Do not play with Fire! Be careful with candles and 'carrying torches'. Always respect and honor your own flame of your body's Life Force; and other's as well. Fire will out devour anything in the Universe. Contained it will cook our food, warm our homes and even be cozy and romantic. However, unleashed and unbridled, (unbridaled?) it can cause pain, death and destruction. Metaphysically, you don't want to be the cause of those things, do you? Do Kiegle pulses, (like stopping the flow of urine), to help activate a release of Life force. Sexual release is also an important part of this Ritual. Direct the power of your orgasm toward the intended purpose. Be Fire! Align with Fire! Increases your Life Force by dancing, moving and gyrating to the Thunder Drums and Horns!

Zaphir

Orange

Ritual of Victory

Amber Fennel Orange

Warming	Gas
Tonic	Acid Stomach
Refreshing	Gout
Weight Loss	Cramps Spasms
Liver Cleanse	Diuretic
PMS	Menopause
Aphrodisiac	Alcoholism
Urinary Discomfort	Depression

Tool: Wand*   **Rune: Tyr=Victory**   **Realm of Mastery**

Stones: Red Rock, Orange calcite, carnelian

Placed: On lower abdomen, back, neck, head to South East.

Phrase: "I wait no More!" (Use your wand!)

Movement: Ocean Depths #9

Music: Flute Oboe Clarinet Reeds

Special Suggestions:

Peel off layers of who you think others want you to be and get down to admitting to the "Real You" even if it sounds silly—who says you can't be a ballerina—translate it into community theater or go for it! Be sure you have your own Wand* to remind you of this part of your Journey—use it often! Learn to direct your focused energies to obtain desired results. What are your intentions? Are they truly honorable, hoping to bring the best for all parties concerned. You can do it! Think it through! Work at it! Then direct your Power!

Delania

Peach   Ritual of Self Defense

Jasmine Patchouli Tangerine

Refreshing	Releases Fears
Aphrodisiac	Balancing Pride
Warming	Courage
Depression	Antiseptic
Uterine Tonic	Nervous Chills
Skin Rejuvenation	Nerve Tonic
Immune Tonic	Wounds

Each time you Journey Peach you are learning to stop Fighting with the past and let your future begin. Be charming and disarming by not being defensive or imagining attacks. Look through the Rooms of Delania's cottage for symbols of triggers.

Tool: Adornments*   Rune: Elks=good fortune   Realm of Mien

Stones: Mongolian Rock Salt, Salmon Marble, Feldspar

Placed: At upper abdomen, back, jaw, head to South East

Phrase: "J am Proud of Myself."

Movement: Gargoyle #8

Music: English Horn

Special Suggestions:

If you'd like to live in a rose covered cottage, plant some roses. Then it's up to you to water, fertilize, spray for aphids etc. Continuously looking to others for support, guidance and rescuing, robs you of the joy and self-esteem of accomplishing those things for yourself. When in Peach some pretty deep-seated fears may surface—just think how proud you'll be of yourself if you can dismantle them and lessen their power over you. Gather all the just right adornments to you, which may help you to have Courage!

Courtheon

Yellow   **Ritual of New Light**

Lemon Chamomile Myrrh

Cleansing	PMS
Acid Stomach	Spasms
Nervousness	Digestion
Soothing	Sinuses
Infections	Mouth Sores
Ulcers	Liver Cleanse
Headaches	Fevers
Coughs	Tummy Soother

Each time you are in Yellow there is a new Enlightenment. Do some deep Tummy Breathing to Expand the diaphragm and Solar Plexus. See your life in a new light and don't' be afraid to change.

Tool: Light/Boxes*   Rune: Ken=Enlightenment   Realm of Matching

Stones: Yellow Calcite, citrine, sulfur (esp. if illness)

Placed: At solar plexus, head, eyes, head to East.

Phrase: "I put down my box and Open!"

Movement: Thru the Gate #2

Music: Flutes, Whistles

Special Suggestions:

Life is a Quest to bring into this Reality your other hidden self; to merge all your wonderful qualities. Be your own Soul Mate and may you be blessed with a wondrous companion. Flickering Firelight, a Mongolian Bowl of Fire* Lamp, Shimmering Sunlight, or Mystickal Moonlight are all-important to this ritual. Gather to you a special Box*—into which you can put symbols of your old beliefs— or things you wish to change and literally "put down your box!" and be open.

Jaedn

Lime Green   Ritual of Now

Lime Lemon Frankincense

Gall Bladder	Fever
Liver	Striving
Acidosis	Refresher
Skin Rejuvenator	Balancing
Coughs	Antiseptic
Digestion	Acceptance
Head Congestion	Nausea

Each time you go to Lime, it seems to be a surprise! Could be some liver/ gall bladder or rib cage discomfort and it usually is connected to something happening right
NOW!

Tool: Well of Desire*/a fountain   Rune: Nyd=Absolutes needs   Realm of Manifestation

Stones: Aventurine, Jade, Green calcite, Prenite

Placed: At the xiphoid-Ribs and Brow, head to North East.

Phrase: "J wish >_____ now."

Movement: Openness #16

Music: Drums Flute Chimes

Special Suggestions:

Wish! But don't strive or obsess if it isn't happening in your time frame, it doesn't mean it won't happen. Continue your journey. Fountains* or bowls of water will enhance this Ritual or your bath, a stream or the ocean. One doesn't land often in Lime! Take this opportunity to review your progress through and your action concerning the issue; especially Motives (Red) and Jntentions (Orange). There can be a painful release and a lot of frustration.

143

Tesque

Green   Ritual of Love

Juniper Pine Clary Sage

Respiration   Kidney Stones
Coughs   Disease Discourager
Catarrh   Hair Tonic
Circulation (especially to heart)   Fluid Retention
Warming   Sore Muscles
Antiseptic   Spasms

Each time you Journey in Green you learn about truly loving in a balanced way. Wanting the best and greatest good for the one you love even if it means letting go of your imagined rights and claims.

Tool: Herbs*   Rune: Mann=Ma(man)kind   Realm of Medicinals

Stones: Emeralds, Malachite, Green Calcite, and Fluorite

Placed: At Chest, back; pelvis, head to North East.

Phrase: "I love who you are."

Movement: Yin Yang #7

Music: Drums

Special Suggestions:

Just keep sending out waves of Love; it changes things and it helps everyone on the planet and please don't stop feeling and sending out love to those who have died—they can still feel it. Gather herbs* and plants to you—have some herbal tea*. Isn't love the greatest Need? Be sure you speak words of acceptance, validation, and encouragement to those in your life. Yes, you are a child of the Universe and you have a right to be here—and so do others. Love others for who they are, even if they are not you!

Jy

Aqua   Ritual of Gifts

Ylang Ylang Clary Sage

Mood lifter	Depression
Hair Tonic	Coughs
Circulation	Sore Throats
Blood Pressure Regulation	Spasms
Aphrodisiac	Excel Skin Rejuvenator
Digestion	Nerve Soother
Sleep Aid	PMS/Menopause
Anger	Guilt

Each time you go into Aqua there are lessons of Play, Work, and Guilt. Don't blame others if you don't get playtime. Go for a walk it costs nothing! Buy some "Bubble stuff" and watch your troubles float away. Play Silly! And Receive the gifts with joy!

Tool: Oil*   Rune: Gyfu=Gift   Realm of Message

Stones: Aquamarine, Turquoise, Shell

Placed: At Shoulders, thighs, head to North East.

Phrase: "Give to me—J receive."

Movement: Wings #6

Music: Drums, Chimes

Special Suggestions:

Ask people you know for things like help, touch, validation. Don't deny them the pleasure and joy of giving it to you—Including spouses and those who have crossed over. Ask your spirit guides, too! Go play! Be sure to apply oils to your body especially the shoulders Remember—self-martyrdom isn't pleasant for anyone; you nor those having to deal with you—. You don't really have the weight of the whole world on your shoulders so stop acting like we are all making you carry it.

Kriel

Blue   Ritual of Joy

Bergamot Balsam Hyssop

Calming	Asthma Help
Soothing to Entire System	Blood Pressure Regulation
Sore Throat	Mucus Lining Soother
Tender Glands	Nose/ Throat
Fevers	Stomach/Bowels
Depression	Sorrow
Antiseptic	Tonic
Heartache	Antiseptic

Each time you go to Blue you work upon self worth. How do you fit in? Measure Up? It starts with the childhood family and friends. What Joy when you find out how much you are really worth to you!

Tool: Crystals* Rune: Birkin=Rebirth Realm of Measure

Stones: Blue Calcite, Blue Topaz, Turquoise, Blue Agate

Placed: at throat, neck, lower abdomen and back, head to North.

Phrase: "My turn to be_____! My Time!"

Movement: Seasons and Cycles #5

Music: Drums

Special Suggestions:

All your timing will be Refined—be aware of all the "whens". When is it your turn to say "NO"—"Yes"—"I'd like it to be_____." Really buy a new timepiece! Maybe it's time to stop procrastinating. Gather all your Wonderful Crystals around you, they speak of the Natural Order and magnetic Fields that organize and structure our patterns. You are a Unique and Indispensable crystalline "Being" in this incredible clockwork Universe.

Daemus

Indigo   Ritual of Night Sky

Rosemary, Dark Musk

Colds	Memory
Coughs	Dreams
Nervousness	Skin Problems
Headaches	Acne/Rashes
TMJ	Mouth Sores
Liver	Spasms
Hair and Skin Care	Mental Fatigue

Each time you Journey to Indigo, Magick is afoot! Otherworldly connections begin to increase. But remember, no one knows what you want to say if you don't.

Tool: Voice/Thoughts Rune: Lagu=flow Realm of Meditation

Stones: Sodalite, Jolite, Sapphire, and Lapis

Placed: At Mouth, jaw, upper abdomen, back; head to North West

Phrase: "Whatever Daemus tells you.

Movement: Searches #4

Music: Piano guitar strings percussion

Special Suggestions:

Free up your imagination—Let it be—Let it soar—Try to make up jokes and riddles. Sing, make up and speak out loud poetry. Spirit Dimensions and Natural Dimensions love Rhythm and Rhyme; speaking in rhyming couplets is very effective. Gather to you crystal balls*, Tarot cards*, Pendulums*, Runes* and other divination tools to help ignite the imagination and incite the psychic Powers. Search for Symbols, believe in signs, omens and dreams. Laugh. Those glimpses of Past Lives you remember are important—believe them, use them, don't let go, but extend yourself to others and other dimensions. Learn how it all matters.

Pryll

Purple

Ritual of Alchemy

Lavender Cedarwood Mint

Relaxes Body	Disease Discourager
Strengthens Nerves	Energy Balancer
Tonic to System	Cleansing
Antiseptic	Fevers
Pain Easer	Nausea
Sinus Congestion	Ear noises and Aches
Fainting	Asthma Help
Mental Fatigue	Shock/Grief

Each time you are in Purple your Power flashes and releases; and if there is a storm!!!—all the better. Make sure you wish Harm to None— Then don't be afraid to vent your hurts and feelings fully in meditation

Tool: Storms/Thunder/   Rune: Feoh=hard won   Realm of Music
   Lightening   acquisitions

Stones: Amethyst, Fluorite, Purple Agate

Placed: at eyes, ears, nose, soar plexus, Head to West.

Phrase: "Arrrggghhh!!!"

Movement: Searches #4

Music: Strings, harp

Special Suggestions:

Play musical instruments or use recordings, this is a Lightening Cracking Thunder Crashing release of your alchemy Powers. Don't be afraid of it—you should feel waves of Power releasing, surging and releasing again—in tears-rage-sorrow or Control. This is the safe place to release; you cannot hurt anyone if you release it here in meditation. You will cause a Physiological, chemical response in your body to your mental stimulus and help clear away emotional debris and toxins.

However if you are truly aligned with Truth, Honor, Justice, Love, Strength, Harmony, Comfort, and Joy you will be adding a great deal of Power in the Spirit Dimension- the Astral Plane—so expect changes to occur.

Fahaltryn

Violet

Ritual of Solitude

Lavender Ylang Ylang Light Musk

Brings Lightness	Disinfecting
Cleansing	Skin Soother
Balancing	Headaches
Eases Worry	Fainting
Nervous Tension	Scattered Thoughts
Migraines	Insomnia
Aphrodisiac	Depression
Blood Pressure Regulation	Antiseptic

Each time you enter into Violet you are dealing with re-alignment-changing the mind—merging extremes to form a balanced truth.

Tool: Staff   Rune: Is=Isolation   Realm of Merging

Stones: Lepidolite, Sugilite, Kumzite,

Placed: at Brow, Ribs, Head to South West

Phrase: "I thank, I thank; again, I thank."

Movement: Moon Faces #12

Music: Strings Violin

Special Suggestions:

A peaceful re-alignment is your stay in Violet. A Time of Transition, emotions sweeten and you may find yourself just wanting to be alone these days. Changing your mind, growing, learning. Be sure you have a special Journey Staff* and mark it in some manner during this Ritual of Safe Passage; a notch a feather, a crystal, a Rune. Remember—when in violet—Truth be Known True colors be shown will apply to you and everyone will see you for who you truly are—will that be a good thing? You are evolving into a more enlightened being by participating in your

OWN Life's Journey. More sovereign, more comforted and comforting, more Joyful and a Bringer of Joy.

Calya

Pink
Ritual of Crowning

Rose Sandalwood

Total Tonic	Skin Tonic
Blood Purifier	Hair Tonic
Head Pressure	Brain Tonic
Thoughts Focus	Blood Pressure Balancer
Heart Tonic	Aphrodisiac
Skin Liver Uterine Tonic	Nausea
Depression	Self-Confidence
Coughs	Spiritual Heightened

Each time you are in Pink You learn more and more of your own Realm and Sovereignty Responsibilities. Are you willing to be the Regal One?

Tool: Self/hair   Rune: Ur=Strength   Realm of Mystery

Stones: Rose Quartz, Rhodacrosite, Rhodonite

Placed: at Crown of Head and Knees Head to South West

Phrase: "J am (Name)."

Movement: Double Helix #10, Protect #15, Shiela na Gig #17

Music: Strings

Special Suggestions:

Get a Crown! A Tiara! A circlet! A hat! You are taking possession, central authority, and rightful responsibility for your own Realm. Not just your Life but your Realm—What will you do with this precious time of your Life in this Nature Plain/ Will you be the Unique Diamond Star you are or will you hide and blame others because you are hidden and shame others because they are not? There is no "role" which is more important or valid or precious than the one that is inscribed in your spirit, on your soul, through your body for you to be. Don't deny or deprive the Universe, the World, Your Realm or Your self of you. We are still a Mystery.

Moon Day

White   Ritual of Stillpoint

Chamomile, Lavender Bergamot

Cleansing   Tummy Soother
Purifying   System Soother
Antiseptic   Relaxing
Catarrh   Skin Tonic
Nervousness   Relieves Anxiety
PMS Cramping   Digestion
Spacey Head   Spiritual Heightened
Headache   Ear Aches

Each time you arrive in white there is a stillness—it surrounds, captivates you, try not to feel threatened or uneasy, just be aware of the Response of Spirit.

Tool: Moonlight   Rune: Wyrd=Destiny Realm of Magick

Stones: Quartz, Druzy Quartz, Diamonds, and Opals

Placed: at above- head and feet, head to Center.

Phrase: "......quiet......"

Movement: Beyond the Beyond #18

Music: Anything

Special Suggestions:

Whatever your Spiritual or Religious belief system this is where you stop, Be Still, and see the Magickal, Blessed Response: Feel Mystical, Feel Loved and Important. Of the 27 or More Dimensions we have and understanding of three and the 4th time, we know about but don't really understand. So many times we are faced with choosing between one or the other. Let us try to understand that the extremes make the whole. We can affect our lives, our Universe; and find our Unique Indispensable Facet in the Multidimensional Network: In White we unite!

Evolve to the level of Co-Creator, Bring Comfort and Joy to the Oneness and the All and when you reach an eclipse, a joining of extremes; it's a Moon Day.

Chapter 9 (from Calya's Chronicles)

Our next few strands were consumed with preparations for the Presentation Ball. One sun linked to the next, learning names of the chieftains and their Realms and we found out that the litany of aMaun we so reverently recited were all Real Beings and all coming to the Ball anxious to meet us!

"Oban is chieftain of the Realm of Movement. It lies way to the South West of the Proper. Here-" Arom pointed to the map. "His clan color is Red. It has the energy of new life force and causes Creativity, drive and ambition." He fairly growled, smiling at us and raising clenched fists over his head for emphasis. And it went on like this for strands every spare moment of every sun, eating a meal, walking the streets in the map room.

"Daemus' consort, Zhe, is sister to Zaphir who is chieftess of Mastery Realm in the Orange-South east that is Owna Island and all that." He chuckled, knowing we must be utterly confused.

"It will all make sense soon, I promise you." And- lest I forget- the etiquette lessons were endless as well. The glass goblet must be kept in the center of your place setting to avoid embarrassment of touching someone else's glass. Phrases to speak and the proper response. The whole question of attire was dealt with by Aless. We shopped and chose and shopped and posed. Non and Dourstan found it quite dreadful as did I after the 3rd mission, the ladies however rallied each time another outing was suggested. My least favorite part of preparing was the dance lessons. It seems they are certain standard dances to mark certain festivities. We needed to learn several, and although my intellect is keen, my will sharp, and my calculations precise; my rhythm is easily distracted and cares not for the way the music is counted rather tripping to its own time- tripping being the descriptive word. Non on the other hand is quite graceful. At the end of the second strand, we learned that escorts were to be chosen for us from the Realms based on our energy configurations.

The aMaun can see the patterns and colors in the space that surrounds each of us. They call it Auric field. We began to be truly excited. Perhaps our most favorite preparation was learning how to eat certain delicacies with the proper utensil. Hiel, long strands of almond flavored noodles; boiled Green Gull eggs-which floated in this odd green jelly substance. Pepper wine; pastries with spiced meat and honey biscuits with berries inside-you *must* break it open in order to eat the berry first, never just bite into it-that would be rude. I'm not sure why-but such is the way with etiquette. Of course it was Arom's favorite part of our lessons as well. And the kitchen was cooking and baking constantly to be sure we were well educated; Arom's orders. A few times each strand we practiced Breathing Ritual with Tolus, but for the most part we didn't see him.

One morning we gathered for breakfast and Calya, out of character, arrived last.

"Good Morning Calya." Aless beamed as she continued serving us, but Calya looked odd –weary.

"Are you alright, Cal?" Door asked, concern in his voice.

"Oh just tired" She smiled, "I guess I'm not sleeping well."

"Tell me Princess." Arom softly questioned.

"It's towards morning-I – well, it sounds strange but –I..." she stammered again, "It feels as though someone is in my room. Very close to me. Not to hurt me..." she added quickly, "but I can't awaken fully-I... it seems like I'm floating and I can sometimes almost hear a voice."

"How long has this been happening?" Our teacher asked stuffing a butter-drenched muffin into his mouth and licking chunks from his fingers. "-Every morning?"

"No—at first occasionally, then every morning for the past four suns now." The seeker answered, thankful for the hot tea in front of her.

Aless entered then with a platter of meats and eggs and a soft smile upon her face, which quickly vanished when she saw the look, her husband gave her—one of guarded concern.

"What is it?" she asked nearly audible.

"Someone is projecting to Calya." Arom answered wiping his mouth. Aless gave a sharp little gasp and we all froze like a tableau waiting for an explanation.

"Really!?" Aless bubbled and giggled and sat down next to Calya grabbing the Princess' arm and with eyes dancing asked, "Who is it? Do you know yet?!"

We at least were relieved that it wasn't something horrible, this projecting, and began to breathe again as Arom smirked and continued eating.

"No—I don't know what you mean." Calya said still fogged.

"What is Projecting?"

"Oh it's the first step in our Courting Ritual. Someone's Spirit is seeking you out to see if you are receptive before making soul contact or physical revelation.

"Oooh! How exciting." Delania squealed.

"Ca-ly-a—someone's seeking you out." she said making a face of joy and wonder.

Non, Door and I were very quiet; we all had our own special feelings for our Princess and romantic could surely be named among them but in this strange land where we really knew no one nor nothing of customs nor whom we could truly trust- this Projecting of Spirit could be dangerous- a trick, an invasion of privacy at any rate.

Calya drank down the hot, sweet tea with a soft smile in her eyes. The Princess, being royalty, had learned well at a young age, to carefully guard her true feelings and minimize emotional reactions. She was one of the best diplomatic negotiators in all of Moeth, rivaling her father; and in this chronicler's opinion, surpassing him.

"Perhaps I should spend the night in your room." Non, ever the Protector, suggested pouring himself and Calya another cup of tea.

Door shot back "I don't think so!" and a glare of protective disdain not trusting even one of our own.

"Cal, this is spooky—don't ya think?" he continued, "someone's disembodied spirit floating around your room while you're asleep trying to make contact." And his eyes widened as he wiggled his fingers in front of her face.

"Well, when you say it like that maybe," Calya answered "but when it's happening..." and her voice trailed off as she seemed to put herself back to the dream to find the words; and Arom continued for her.

"...It's the softest, sweetest, longing you've ever known." And Calya just nodded and smiled lowering her eyes to her plate with an expression of disbelief upon her face.

Aless gave a sharp little gasp again

"She is receptive" she breathed, and made a mental note to keep a very watchful eye on everyone.

After that breakfast, we went for clothing fittings and dance lessons—again. And with all the hours of those strands filled, we scarcely had had time to talk with each other, just the five.

Tolus the trickster; for that name which we had used all our lives and which flows so easily from the tongue was hard to relinquish; had not been present at the Courtheon. We were told that as Regal Lord of all Hammeril, he had many matters of State and estates to attend. So Arom, later that same sun, had left us to do Breathing Ritual on our own—we had become that accomplished at it. Of course, left on our own we began well, but immediately fell into hungrily conversing for as I have said, we had not had many private moments together since we arrived.

Door was the first to break the silence.

"So what do you all really think of this place?" he asked sitting up and making sure no one else was around to hear. Sitting up as well, I answered,

"I find it a wonder. New flora and fauna to study, the aMaun are a remarkable people."

"People?"—Delania interrupted, amazement on her face,

"They're not like aMaun they are just like us—almost—"

"They have strong powers—" Non said softly without looking up.

"We are outnumbered and by beings who out power us beyond our dreams."

We all looked at him in awe waiting for some added calming explanation of his observation.

He sighed heavily as if he couldn't believe we didn't understand and sat up to face us.

"They can transport things and people with their minds!" he continued, "who knows what else they can do? They are <u>not</u> like us."

Calya added, "They are aMaun—we need to remember that. And that we don't really know them."

At that moment we were all startled by the appearance of the Regal Lord. He stepped from behind a pillar and might have been there all along—we just couldn't be sure. That was the feeling we were beginning to have about many things in Hammeril.

"Arom seems to think you are all deep in meditation with the Breathing Ritual. Now I wonder where he got such an idea?"

Tolus scolded in feigned scolding and we all felt like we'd been caught in the creamery.

Calya began "My friends and I have scarce had a time to..."

"This is the time to do Breathing Ritual!" Tolus interrupted. "You can exchange pleasantries later."

"Except there never seems to be a later." Calya's voice was sharp with her point.

"You are here to learn..."

"We are on a mission—a quest to find..."

"The Wise Ways—" the Regal Lord loudly finished for her.

"I know—and we are here to teach you." He bowed arms spread widely.

"I beg your pardon, sir" I ventured cautiously, "but all we seem to be doing is shopping for clothes."

"Yeah—what d'ye say to that?" Door snapped curtly. "That's not what we came here to do."

"Actually..." Tolus smirked as he leaned against the pillar and folded his arms "it is part of it, and you all could use a few more outings it would appear." He eyed us with seeming displeasure.

I, and we all heard Delania's soft little voice whisper to Calya

"I don't mind, do you?" and the Regal Lord turned quickly away from us. At first I thought in annoyance but he cleared his throat and I think he laughed.

"As I have said—" Calya continued, gathering herself, "our quest is of the utmost importance to us, and we are still a bit unsure of what it is we are supposed to be learning."

"Exactly, Princess" Tolus countered, his tone a bit condescending, "so why not calm down and let us teach you our wisdom which we know how to do very well? You need to put down your box—"

"I think we are remaining very calm –sir." Calya stood to face him squarely, "and besides your Breathing Ritual which we have mastered, we have yet to be taught much of anything."

"Mastered!" Tolus shouted truly angered this time. "You've barely grasped hold of it, not 'mastered' Princess Calya-tril of Moeth!" And he was gone in a flash of soft golden light, his words hanging in the air and Calya's diminuative name echoing as if it were a profanity.

After many remarks of disbelief, dislike, and distrust—the others soon departed the room. I could hear them talking of Tolus' arrogance and Calya's strength but as for me I had a mind for exploring. All throughout the Courtheon were intricately connected, carefully concealed passageways. One could pass unnoticed to any other place in the Great building by walking through the spaces and tunnels between the walls, even gong up and down stairs by means of hidden stairways. Sometimes, the people in the room could easily be observed and overheard by standing with in a wall or under a floor. I was learning my way around and becoming quite adept at my newfound talent.

And that, dear reader, is how I came to over hear the conversation I will next report here; although at the time I was keeping my sleuthing and the secrets I gathered to myself.

As I have said, the others had gone off and I went through the Ritual room to a small room of mixing at the back where supplies were kept and off that was another room, even smaller, with a well distinguished sliding door which connected to the corridor system. I had found it while searching for the privy and it had been the beginning of my sleuthing.

I entered the passage and moved carefully and quietly. This time I came to a wall grating in the Baths I remembered seeing while bathing. I looked from the other side.

Tolus and Arom were relaxing in the steam pool—their bodies relaxed I should say; however, their conversation was becoming heated.

"I have no time for this Arom. I am a very busy man. They are not the ones for whom we wait—they cannot be."

"They are the 5-who-come-seeking." Arom said emphatically, "they came through the archway on Garden Island, they speak of Moeth, and call Calya the Seeker. She is the daughter of Moeth and Gwiltryn; surely there is no doubt in your mind of that! Those eyes," he added smiling "like the color of blue berries.

That hair, no denying Gwiltryn there—the abundance, the soft, sable curls—"

"She ought to have her head shaved—" Tolus muttered and sank down under the water. When he surfaced, Arom continued smirking.

"Does she trouble you that greatly?" he asked, brows raised. The Regal Lord looked sternly at the Elder aMaun who sat with him in the healing waters.

"They are all more trouble than they are worth." Tolus said in a measured cadence.

"I don't have time to teach them the Ways of Refinement. You and Aless are better suited to that." He dunked under again and resurfaced quickly wiping water from his face

"She thinks she has mastered the Breathing Ritual" he scoffed loudly.

Arom answered quietly "they don't know what they don't know Toli. You need to put down your box."

There was that phrase again—Tolus had spoken it to Calya.

I noted to ask Arom it's meaning.

"Where the dresn Boh is Gim." Tolus muttered as he slipped under the hot waters again for the third time and Arom eased into a comfortable position a victorious and satisfied smile on his face. And at that instant, Gim hurried in golden hair in his face and a sky blue robe wrapped around him several times. He stood over the pool as Tolus surfaced and said loudly in mock displeasure,

"About time you came up for air—we've a meeting here you know" and he dropped off his robe and entered the steam pool.

"One could say the same to you—" Tolus quipped, "you and Beryl haven't come up for air or food or light since you return."

"We've circuits to make up for Tolus circuits. You know that. 36 to be exact." Gim sank down under the water for a heartbeat then resurfaced.

Tolus looked at him with a darkened mood.

"Not scolding, Gim—just envious" and all 3 of them smiled wearily. I noted that Gim's body looked firm and young—certainly not the body of the feeble, shriveled old Gim of the Luminaries shop and duly assumed it was a different Gim.

Arom took his turn dunking and after he surfaced, loudly exclaimed, "Beryl! Beryl! Such a precious gem—you should get yourself one of those, Toli."

"I tried," Tolus smirked "she said she'd prefer to wait for Gim to return."

The two friends eyed each other silently, cautiously, and then Gim grinned,

"She's not just a beautiful woman, she's a wise woman too; with impeccable taste."

We all chuckled and I was afraid I was found out but they continued.

Arom said,

"What's the word from the Zahain, Gim? Any progress?"

"No, not good—" Gim answered. "Negotiations are falling apart. Those dresn Helmets want to just push in and take everything. I think it's time the Regal Lord makes an appearance."

Tolus rubbed the back of his neck.

"As if I don't have enough to do" he moaned, "two suns—no," he corrected, closing his eyes and checking a mental calendar, "three suns; I'll come up—maybe." Then to Arom,

"We need to start the five on transing and maybe foujon—and—" he sighed and groaned again "this dresn Presentation Ball." He sank slowly beneath the steaming water as Arom informed Gim,

"Tolus doesn't believe that these are the five for whom we've been waiting."

Gim sat motionless but I could tell anger was seething in him. Then, as Tolus surfaced, a powerful wave surged across the pool and caught him off guard, as did the torrent of angry words from his friend.

"What the dresn Boh do you mean not the five!?" Gim shouted, his face contorting as he spat out the words. Tolus gasped and choked as he tried to recover from the water down his throat.

"I was there! I waited—alone! Moeth and the other exiles didn't even know me—remember? Do you have any idea how quickly we age there? I watched myself wither and shrivel thinking I might die before she was found—waiting for Moeth to name her—I could do nothing. I saw the 25 exiles die off, one-by-one never remembering fully who they were—never returning home!" His face released and his eyes grew sad.

"252 Calaithian circuits. Watching generation after generation of the Calaithians be born, grow old, and die without the Refinements, without knowing what their lives are truly about—being the only one there for 252 circuits who knew of the Reality of the Realms and the truth about the Exiles. You stayed here—living your lives—I- was- there!" he said emphatically, "and Calya is the One!"

"You chose to go." Tolus said, his voice hard.

"Who else would have?" Gim asked softly and there was silence. Then he continued,

"You did what you had to do. We all know that Tol. The agreement was fair and ratified by the aDrohl—by Boh and aMaelun. And you made sure there would be one found who could reunite all the Realms again and make peace. Calya is the One, Tol. I knew it the night she was born. I felt the energy shift. I've watched her grow. She has a gentle compassionate spirit;

she's willing to learn, willing to seek, to find, to open, to use for the Love of One and the Good of All. Just like you ordered."

Gim sank beneath the hot waters very slowly and carefully seeming to wish not to make any more ripples and I realized our Gim, he truly was.

When he came up, Tolus abruptly climbed out of the pool calling back angrily,

"She's Moeth's daughter! And I want nothing to do with her!"

"But the agreement—?" Gim shouted.

Dres the agreement!" the Regal Lord turned angrily to face the two in the pool with tiny bright sparks bristling, glinting, in circles all around him. Neither Arom nor Gim moved nor said a word as Tolus turned to stride away. Then Gim called after him,

"So, if you'd show up at the Zahain as mad as you are now— you know, as a fireball or a lightning bolt or something—"

Tolus spun sharply about yelling,

"Then you would have just spent 252 agonizing circuits in Calaith for nothing!" and he disappeared in a bright blue flash. There was silence with only the splash of residual waves to be heard Arom and Gim began to mutter.

Gim: "He's right—"

Arom: "Of course he's right."

Gim: "Moeth's daughter" he humphed.

Arom: "Ironic isn't it? The aDrohl do have a sense of humor."

Then I thought I heard someone in the corridor so I hurried back to join the rest of the five.

Journey-Wise

Calýa Journey-Wise P.O. Box 802. Hope Valley, RI 02832-0802.

Calya Journey-wise products and support items may be obtained at your local shops and bookstores and at:
Pelham Grayson Inc., 1-800-321-8725 ex 205.
Website: pelhamgrayson.com

ᏅAn Anointing Ritual Treatment consists of a thorough consultation including led Calya Meditation, and Intuitive Understanding to help in determining imbalances. Then, a Calya Aromatherapy Myst with appropriate blends, Journey-wise chapter work, and soothing hot stones for clearing and directing proper energy flow as you Journey the Realms with a final releasing meditation.

Calýa Courses

Courses in Metaphysical Arts, including Certifications in Holistic Aromatherapy, Divinations, Calýa Journey-Wise system of Metaphysical Wellness are available as workshops.   1-800-321-8725, ex 205

I. Holistic Aromatherapy   **200 hrs.**
   a. History & Traditions   f. Chemistry
   b. Mind/Body Connections   g. Affinities/Keneisiology
   c. Essential Oils/Data   h. Anointings/Reflexology
   d. Body Systems/Types   i. Blending/Sanitation
   e. Charting Imbalance   j. Legalities/Exams
      Preparation for National Registry Council Board Exam
      Aromatherapy
            (includes II. Basic Journey -Wise)

II. Basic Journey-Wise   **20 hrs.**
   a. 17 Realms   e. Balance Line
   b. Vibrational Frequencies   f. Quest Chapters
   c. Meditations   g. Releasing/Transmuting
   d. Foods/Blends/Crystals   h. Breathing/Moving
            (Workbook Required)

III. Celtic Spirit & Divinations   **40 hrs.**
   a. History of ImRam, Myths   e. Tarot & Scrying
   b. Psychic Development   f. Crystals & Spells
   c. Spirit Art   g. Dreams & Past Lives
   d. Runes, Trees, Totems   h. Ethics/Harm None

IV. Certification in Calýa   Journey-wise 200hrs

a. the Journey Guide	f. Sanitation	k. Listen/Think
b. 17 Realms	g. Anointing Rituals	l. Omens
c. Body/Soul/Spirit	h. Guides & Meditation	m. Stillpoints
d. Charting Imbalances	i. Pendulums/ Ear Cones	n. The Chronicles
e. Consultations	j. Crystal Powers	o. Ethics

(This may be combined with other courses)

Each Student is Required to Contract for Classes and to continue ad infinitum to maintain the name practices and integrity of the Calýa Journey-wise System, Method and Products.

Always this is an energetic Spiritual Journey and should not be deemed more than it is. Calya Journey-wise is never meant to replace professional counseling or the advice of your Health care provider.

Safe Passage and Journey-wise!

About the Author

Catherine L. Avizinis (Calya) lives the metaphysical mystical life about which she teaches and writes. The system is the result of years of intuitive counseling and healing practice which is now centered at Celtic Moon Hol-Health Center, which itself is a result of her own Journey-work.

Journey guide to many, she is also wife of 27 years, mother of three fine sons, musician, artist, licensed cosmetologist, herbologist, cert. To teach Legal Russian Ballet, dance and movement, Cert. Holistic Aromatherapist, instructor, developer of the Calya system and Aromatherapy line.

Printed in the United States
18380LVS00001B/171-180